PEA
Round the World Quiz Book
Gyles Brandreth

PELHAM BOOKS

First published in Great Britain by
PELHAM BOOKS LTD
52 Bedford Square
London WC1B 3EF
1978

Copyright © 1978 Victorama Limited

Designed by John Elsegood

All Rights Reserved. No part of this publication
may be reproduced, stored in a retrieval system,
or transmitted, in any form or by any means,
electronic, mechanical, photocopying, recording
or otherwise, without the prior permission
of the Copyright owner.

ISBN 0 7207 1110 X

Printed and bound in Great Britain by
Hollen St. Press Ltd., Slough

**To Nina Tsihlakis
a good friend**

SOME OTHER BOOKS BY GYLES BRANDRETH

Quiz Books
PEARS FAMILY QUIZ BOOK
PEARS ALL THE YEAR ROUND QUIZ BOOK
THE ROYAL QUIZ BOOK
THE GENERATION QUIZ BOOK

Family Entertainment
COMPLETE BOOK OF HOME ENTERTAINMENT
BRANDRETH'S PARTY GAMES
GAMES FOR TRAINS, PLANES AND WET DAYS
BRANDRETH'S CHRISTMAS BOOK
BRANDRETH'S BOOK OF WAITING GAMES
KNIGHT BOOK OF SCRABBLE
TEACH YOURSELF INDOOR GAMES
THE LITTLE RED DARTS BOOK

General Books
CREATED IN CAPTIVITY
DISCOVERING PANTOMIME
I SCREAM FOR ICE CREAM
BRANDRETH'S BEDROOM BOOK
A ROYAL SCRAPBOOK
YAROOH!
THE FUNNIEST MAN ON EARTH
THE MAGIC OF HOUDINI
THE COMPLETE HUSBAND

Children's Books
KNIGHT BOOK OF PARTY GAMES
KNIGHT BOOK OF CHRISTMAS FUN
KNIGHT BOOK OF EASTER FUN
KNIGHT BOOK OF HOSPITAL FUN AND GAMES
KNIGHT BOOK OF MAZES
KNIGHT BOOK OF HOLIDAY FUN AND GAMES
KNIGHT BOOK OF FUN AND GAMES FOR JOURNEYS
KNIGHT BOOK OF FUN AND GAMES FOR A RAINY DAY
NUMBER GAMES AND PUZZLES
PAPER AND PENCIL GAMES AND PUZZLES
DOMINO GAMES AND PUZZLES
GAMES AND PUZZLES WITH COINS AND MATCHES

FUN AND GAMES FOR EVERY DAY OF THE YEAR
THE HOW AND WHY BUMPER WONDER BOOK
HOTCHPOTCH
BRAINTEASERS AND MINDBENDERS
PROJECT: CASTLES AND HISTORIC HOUSES
PARTY GAMES FOR YOUNG CHILDREN
EDWARD LEAR'S BOOK OF MAZES
BE KIND TO MUM AND DAD
TONGUE-TWISTERS
THE BIG BOOK OF SECRETS
THE PUZZLE PARTY FUN BOOK
THE DAFT DICTIONARY
WHAT NONSENSE!
CRAZY CROSSWORDS
BEAVER BOOK OF MAGIC
JOKES! JOKES! JOKES!
THE GREAT BIG FUNNY BOOK
THE GREAT GAMES GAZETTE
SPYFILE

Contents

Introduction page 8
Questions page 13
Answers page 193

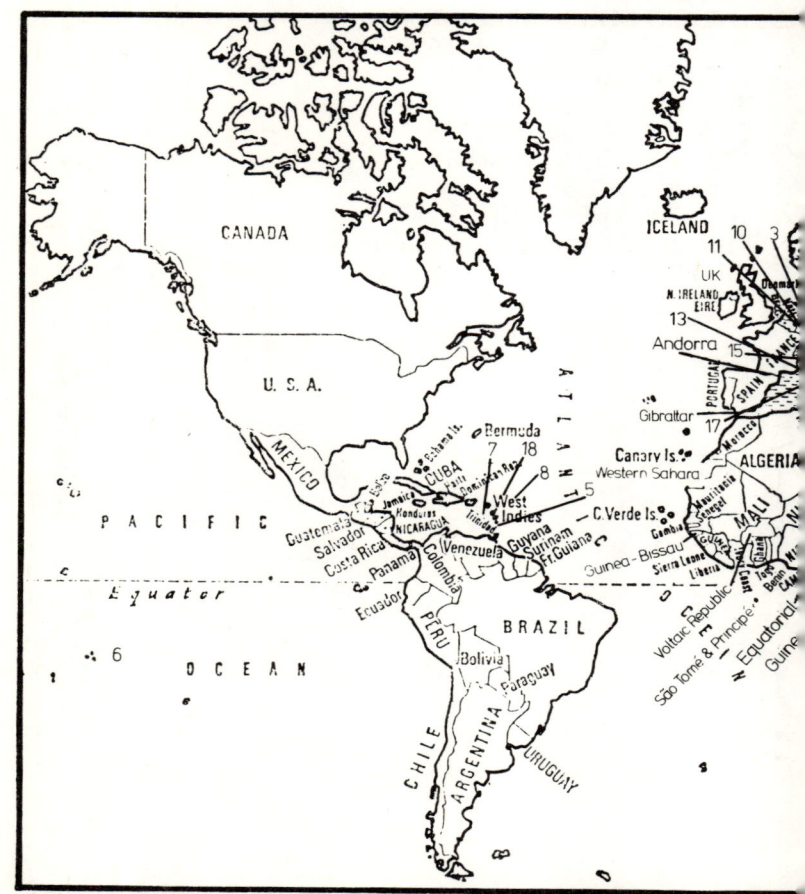

1	Madagascar	6	Fr Polynesia
2	Albania	7	Grenada
3	Austria	8	Guadeloupe
4	Bahrain	9	Kampuchea
5	Barbados	10	Liechtenstein

11 Luxembourg
12 Malaysia
13 Monaco
14 Qatar
15 San Marino
16 United Arab Emirates
17 Vatican City
18 Virgin Is

Introduction

Though I say it as shouldn't, this quiz book is unique. To be sure, there have been other first-class quiz books – the *Pears Family Quiz Book* and the *Pears All the Year Round Quiz Book* are two classics of the *genre* that spring immediately to mind – but there has never, ever (no, not *ever*) been a quiz book quite like this one.

The reason, of course, is that this quiz book isn't just a quiz book: it's a trip around the world, a once-in-a-lifetime chance to visit every country on earth. You can start where you want and go where you like – and all the baggage you need you're already carrying in your head. This world cruise is the globe-trotter's dream: no lost luggage, no running out of foreign currency, no visas, no inoculations, no gippy tummy.

And, not content with being your passport to the world, the book is also a game. The rules are simple:

1. Choose the country where you would most like to start your world tour and go there. (There is a quiz for each country and they appear in alphabetical order, from Afghanistan on page 19 to Zimbabwe on page 191.)

2. When you have found your country, answer all three questions given. Real Masterminds will be able to answer the questions without looking at the list of four alternative answers printed below each question. If you think you may be a Mastermind, cover up the four alternatives until you've given your answer. If you're not so confident, pick the alternative you think most likely. You can check the correct answers at the back of the book. If you are awarding yourself marks, you get five for every question you answer correctly immediately, but only one for the

questions you answer after you have been given the four alternatives.

3. When you have answered all three questions, look at the choice of countries surrounding you, listed at the foot of the page under the heading WHERE NEXT? and move on to one of them.

4. You can't go to the same country twice, so if you find you've already visited all the countries listed under WHERE NEXT? you're free to go to any other country you happen to fancy.

5. If you feel inclined, you can keep track of your transworld journeyings by marking off the countries you visit on the map on pages 10 and 11.

6. When you've been to every country, sit back, congratulate yourself and reflect on what a small world we live in.

Reflect too on the fact that it's a changing world. The information used in preparing the quiz questions has been culled from those two redoubtable volumes, *Pears Cyclopaedia* and *Junior Pears Encyclopaedia*, which means that it's as accurate and up-to-date as possible, but between my preparing the book and your getting hold of it, governments may have toppled and countries changed their borders and their names. If I've given the population of Madagascar as 7,550,000, but you happen to know it's really 7,601,438, don't write and complain: alas, funds did not allow me to visit the place in person to count all the legs on the island and divide them by two. I've simply had to rely on the latest available statistics.

And, while I've tried to be as comprehensive as possible, there may be one or two outlandish spots I've forgotten to include. If I've omitted France or China (I haven't) I'll accept your protestations with a good grace, but if I've slipped up on the Comoro Islands (I think I have) I trust you'll forgive me.

Bon voyage!

When you have visited a country and completed its quiz, mark it here:

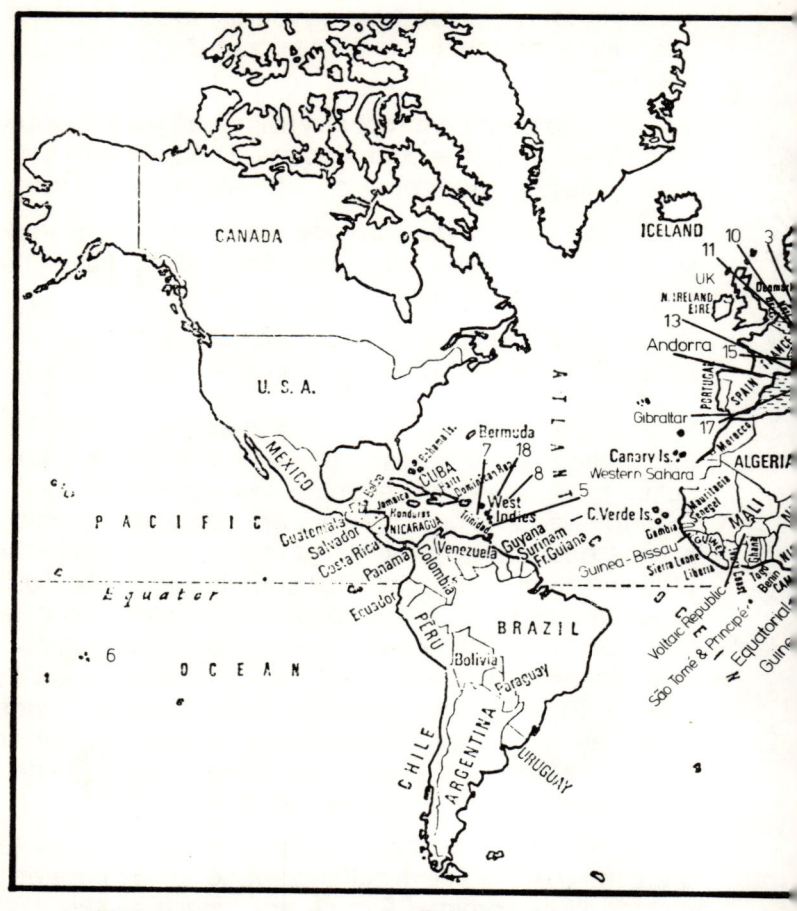

1	Madagascar	6	Fr Polynesia
2	Albania	7	Grenada
3	Austria	8	Guadeloupe
4	Bahrain	9	Kampuchea
5	Barbados	10	Liechtenstein

11 Luxembourg
12 Malaysia
13 Monaco
14 Qatar
15 San Marino
16 United Arab Emirates
17 Vatican City
18 Virgin Is

Questions

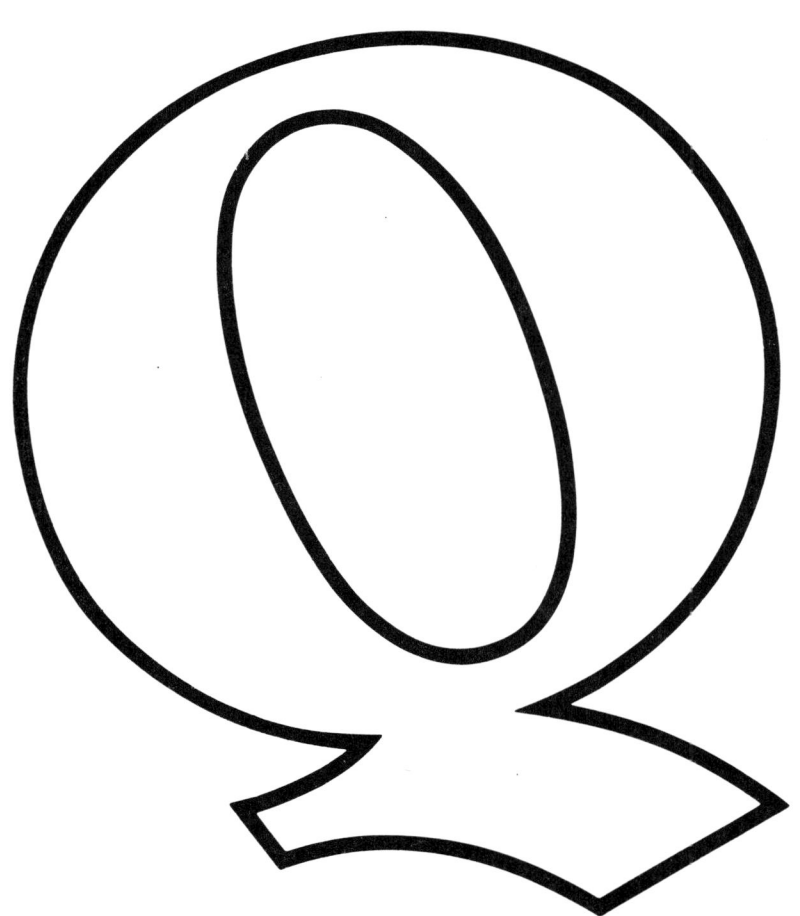

What a World!

Before you set off on your round-the-world expedition here are ten quick questions to put you in the mood.

1. **The world's largest island covers an area of nearly three million square miles. What's it called?**
    Greenland?
    Iceland?
    Australia?
    Borneo?

2. **Over 2,000 different languages are spoken in the world today. One of those languages is spoken by almost 500,000,000 people. It is the world's most popular language. What is it?**
    English?
    Hindi?
    Mandarin Chinese?
    Spanish?

3. **Of the world's oceans, one is by far the largest. It covers nearly 64,000,000 square miles – more than twice the area covered by the world's second largest ocean. What is the largest ocean called?**
    The Arctic?
    The Pacific?
    The Atlantic?
    The Indian?

4. **What was the name of the Viking who discovered Greenland in 982?**
    Leif Ericsson
    Eric the Red?
    Marco Polo?
    Christopher Columbus?

5. **Who was the first navigator to sail around the world in 1519–1522?**
    Sebastian Cabot?
    Ferdinand Magellan?
    Francis Drake?
    Clare Francis?

6. **Roughly what percentage of the earth's surface is covered with water?**
    30%?
    50%?
    70%?
    89%?

7. **The earth, which weighs some 6,588,000,000,000,000,000,000 tons, is the fifth largest of the major planets. How many major planets are there?**
    Five?
    Nine?
    Eleven?
    Twenty-six?

8. **New York and Tokyo are the world's two most populated cities, with populations of over 11,000,000. What is the world's third most populated city?**
    Shanghai?
    London?
    Buenos Aires?
    Cleethorpes?

9. **'Cumulus', 'stratus', 'cirrus' are very much features of the world in which we live. What are they?**
    The layers that form the earth's outer crust?
    Latin names for the world's principal seas?
    The three most widespread diseases currently known to man: i.e. the common cold, influenza and the measles?
    Clouds?

10. The rest of the book is an A to Z of the countries of the world, from Afghanistan right the way through to Zimbabwe. If it had been an A to Z of all the *places*, we would have had to start at the Danish port of Aabenraa and gone all the way through to Zwolle. Where is Zwolle?
> Zambia?
> Peru?
> Poland?
> The Netherlands?

And now that you've had the shrimp cocktail as your starter, the world is your oyster – but remember: you mustn't just work your way through from A to Z. You must choose a country to begin in and make your round-the-world trip from there.

Afghanistan

1. **What is the population of Afghanistan?**
    Over six million?
    Over nineteen million?
    Over thirty-three million?
    Over sixty million?

2. **In 1973 Muhammad Daoud seized power in Afghanistan and declared the country a republic with himself as President. What happened to Daoud in the spring of 1978? Was he:**
    Elected President for life?
    Forced to flee to West Pakistan after a military coup?
    Overthrown and assassinated?
    Defeated in the country's first-ever general election?

3. **What is the name of the currency used in Afghanistan?**
    The dollar?
    The kurd?
    The kabul?
    The afghani?

    WHERE NEXT?

    Soviet Union, Iran or Pakistan.

Albania

1. **What is the capital of Albania?**
    Riga?
    Tirana?
    Belgrade?
    Shkoder?

2. **Albania was once a province of which great Empire?**
    The British Empire?
    The Holy Roman Empire?
    The Ottoman Empire?
    The Roman Empire?

3. **Between 1928 and 1939 who was King of Albania?**
    King Paul IV?
    King Constantine III?
    King Rudolf?
    King Zog?

WHERE NEXT?

Yugoslavia or Greece.

Algeria

1. When was the first French conquest of Algeria?
    1617?
    1790?
    1830?
    1911?

2. When General de Gaulle of France proclaimed Algeria independent in 1962, who was first elected President?
    Ben Bella?
    Ferhat Abbas?
    Houari Boumédienne?
    Albert Camus?

3. The armed forces of Algeria number over 60,000 men. From which country does most of their military equipment come?
    France?
    The Soviet Union?
    Libya?
    The United States?

WHERE NEXT?

Morocco, Mauritania, Mali, Niger, Libya or Tunisia.

American Samoa

1. **When were the Samoan Islands discovered and by whom?**
   The Dutch in 1722?
   The Spanish in 1590?
   The British in 1804?
   The Americans in 1889?

2. **Since 1899 Eastern Samoa has been called American Samoa. What is its relationship with the United States?**
   The 46th American state?
   An American colony?
   An Independent American Protectorate?
   Totally independent of the United States?

3. **Apart from English, what is the main language spoken in American Samoa?**
   Polynesian?
   Samoan?
   Papuan?
   French?

WHERE NEXT?

Western Samoa, Australia or New Zealand.

Andorra

1. **Andorra is an independent principality. It has two princes. Who are they?**
   Prince Emmanuel II and Prince Rainier IV?
   Prince Carl-Gustaf and Prince Max von Sydow?
   Prince Anders and Prince Charles?
   The President of France and the Spanish Bishop of Urgel?

2. **What is the population of Andorra?**
   About 16,000?
   About 160,000?
   About 260,000?
   About 1,600,000?

3. **What was the name of the Austrian playwright who wrote a play called *Andorra* that was presented by the National Theatre Company at the Old Vic in London in the 1960s?**
   Bertholt Brecht?
   Friedrich Dürrenmatt?
   Max Frisch?
   Heinrich Boll?

WHERE NEXT?

Spain or France.

Angola

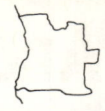

1. **What is the capital of Angola?**
   Brazzaville?
   Lobito?
   Silva Porto?
   Luanda?

2. **Until 11 November 1975, Angola was an 'overseas province' of which European country?**
   Spain?
   Portugal?
   France?
   Italy?

3. **The military intervention of which countries secured the rule of the Marxist M.P.L.A. People's Democracy in Angola in 1976?**
   The Soviet Union and Egypt?
   Zaïre and Zambia?
   The Soviet Union and Cuba?
   China and Namibia?

WHERE NEXT?

Namibia, Zambia, Zaïre or Congo.

Argentina

1. **The capital of Argentina is Buenos Aires. When was the city founded?**
    1536?
    1789?
    1850?
    1910?

2. **Argentina is the world's largest exporter of which product?**
    Grain?
    Silk?
    Meat?
    Oranges?

3. ***Evita*, the musical about Eva Peron whose husband became President of Argentina in 1946, opened in London in the summer of 1978. At which theatre?**
    The Theatre Royal, Drury Lane?
    Her Majesty's?
    The Globe?
    The Prince Edward?

WHERE NEXT?

Chile, Bolivia, Paraguay or Uruguay.

Australia

1. **What is the capital of Australia?**
    Sydney?
    Melbourne?
    Hobart?
    Canberra?

2. **What was the name of the Australian Prime Minister who was drowned in 1967?**
    Gough Whitlam?
    John Gorton?
    William McMahon?
    Harold Holt?

3. **What proportion of the Australian population is Aboriginal?**
    1%?
    10%?
    18%?
    31%?

WHERE NEXT?

Papua New Guinea, American Samoa, Western Samoa, or New Zealand.

Austria

1. **In which Viennese city was the composer Mozart born?**
   Vienna?
   Graz?
   Salzburg?
   Innsbruck?

2. **When was the first Austrian Republic created?**
   1600?
   1880?
   1914?
   1918?

3. **What is the name of Austria's main waterway?**
   The Essen?
   The Volga?
   The Danube?
   The Anton?

WHERE NEXT?

Italy, Switzerland, West Germany, Czechoslovakia, Hungary or Yugoslavia.

Bahamas

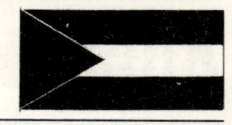

1. **The Bahamas were Columbus's first American discovery. In what year?**
   1415?
   1492?
   1521?
   1604?

2. **The Bahamas cover a total area of 4,404 square miles, but of the hundreds of islands, rocks and cays in the archipelago how many are inhabited?**
   About 20?
   About 40?
   About 60?
   About 80?

3. **Britain granted the Bahamas independence in 1973. Who is now the Bahamian Head of State?**
   Premier Lynden O. Pinding?
   President Bimini S. Brown?
   Sir Milo B. Butler?
   Queen Elizabeth II?

WHERE NEXT?

The United States, Cuba or Haiti.

Bahrain

1. **Until the discovery of oil in 1932, what was the industry for which Bahrain was famous?**
   White slave trading?
   Sardine cultivation?
   Pearl fishing?
   Textile manufacturing?

2. **The discovery of oil in Bahrain transformed the sheikdom's economy. When is the oil expected to run out?**
   Never?
   In 1990?
   In 2050?
   In 3000?

3. **In 1970 which country referred its claim to being the rightful owners of Bahrain to the United Nations? The claim was later dropped.**
   Iran?
   Saudi Arabia?
   Qatar?
   Kuwait?

WHERE NEXT?

Saudi Arabia, Iran or Qatar.

Bangladesh

1. **The 1971 war of independence led to East Pakistan becoming Bangladesh and the hero of the struggle against Pakistan became Prime Minister in January 1972. What was his name?**
    Yahya Khan?
    Ali Bhutto?
    Sheikh Mujib?
    Ayub Khan?

2. **Three years later, in January 1975, the Prime Minister made himself President and gave himself absolute powers. He lost power in August 1975. How? Was he:**
    Overthrown by General Ziar Rahman?
    Murdered by a group of army majors?
    Deported to India?
    Overwhelmingly defeated in the general election he was forced to call?

3. **Bangladesh provides 80 per cent of the world market of what commodity?**
    Jute?
    Tea?
    Sugar cane?
    Timber?

WHERE NEXT?

India or Burma.

Barbados

1. The English landed in Barbados in 1605 and the island was granted independence in 1966. Its parliament is a House of Assembly with 24 members. How far back does the House of Assembly date?
    1966?
    1918?
    1850?
    1639?

2. Is Barbados:
    The most westerly of the West Indies?
    The most easterly of the West Indies?
    The most northerly of the West Indies?
    The most southerly of the West Indies?

3. What important product did Barbados supply to the Royal Navy for centuries until 1970?
    Rope used in rigging?
    Gun metal?
    Magnesium?
    Rum?

WHERE NEXT?

Trinidad and Tobago, Grenada or the Virgin Islands.

Belgium

1. **When did Belgium gain its independence from the Netherlands?**
   - 1790?
   - 1830?
   - 1890?
   - 1945?

2. **Some 60 per cent of the Belgian population comes from Germanic stock and are known as Flemings. About 40 per cent of the population comes from French stock. How are they known?**
   - Brussellois?
   - Flamandes?
   - Ardennese?
   - Walloons?

3. **In 1951, at the age of 21, Baudouin I became King of Belgium. Why?**
   - His father, King Leopold III, died?
   - His father, King Leopold III, was assassinated?
   - His father, King Leopold III, abdicated in his favour?
   - He overthrew his father?

WHERE NEXT?

The Netherlands, West Germany, Luxembourg or France.

Belize

1. **How was Belize known before 1972?**
    Martinique?
    The Cayman Islands?
    Portuguese West Indies?
    British Honduras?

2. **In 1638 who were Belize's first settlers?**
    Spanish pirates?
    Portuguese explorers?
    The French navy?
    Shipwrecked English sailors?

3. **When British troops arrived in Belize in 1972 to carry out military exercises, their arrival caused a major diplomatic row with a country that maintains it has a claim to Belize. Which country?**
    Mexico?
    Guatemala?
    Nicaragua?
    Cuba?

WHERE NEXT?

Guatemala or Mexico.

Benin

1. **Throughout most of the country's history, what was Benin's name?**
    Togo?
    Yoruba?
    Chad?
    Dahomey?

2. **Tourists visiting Benin often visit Natitingou and Ouidah. For what features are these centres famous?**
    Diamond mines?
    Game reserves?
    Prehistoric wall paintings?
    Black magic?

3. **Benin covers an area of some 44,910 square miles. What is its population?**
    Over 3,000,000?
    Over 13,000,000?
    Over 30,000,000?
    Over 130,000,000?

WHERE NEXT?

Togo, Voltaic Republic, Niger or Nigeria.

Bermuda

1. **How did Bermuda get its name?**
    It was discovered by Juan Bermudez in 1503?
    'Ber' and 'muda' are two Caribbean words meaning 'beautiful islands'?
    Sir Edwin Bermuda was the islands' first Governor-General?
    The islands are on the same latitude as Burma, but much smaller, Bermuda meaning 'Little Burma'?

2. **In 1941 the British granted the United States a 99-year lease on the Bermuda naval base. The area of Bermuda is only 20.6 square miles. The naval base takes up 2.3 square miles. Why did Britain give the United States the lease?**
    For President Roosevelt's sixtieth birthday present?
    In return for the United States paying off Britain's war debt?
    In return for an American promise to enter the war in Europe?
    In return for destroyers needed for anti-submarine operations?

3. **What are 'Bermudas'?**
    Cocktails containing rum and vodka?
    Bikini briefs?
    Mountain goats found on the islands?
    Long shorts?

    WHERE NEXT?

    United States or the Bahamas.

Bhutan

1. **What kind of Head of State does Bhutan have?**
    An hereditary monarch?
    An elected President?
    A military dictator?
    A Governor appointed by the Indian government?

2. **What is the principal religion of Bhutan?**
    Christianity?
    Mahayana Buddhism?
    Muslim?
    Hindu?

3. **What foreign power claims a 300-square-mile sector of Bhutan along the country's eastern border?**
    India?
    China?
    Sikkim?
    Nepal?

    WHERE NEXT?

    China or India.

Bolivia

1. To find the oldest church in use in South America you would travel to the capital of Bolivia, which is not La Paz, which is the seat of government. What is the name of Bolivia's capital city?
    Santa Cruz?
    Potosi?
    Cochabamba?
    Sucre?

2. When was Bolivia liberated from Spain?
    1790?
    1825?
    1890?
    1930?

3. What was the name of the internationally famous Bolivian guerrilla leader killed in 1967?
    Juan Peron?
    Hugo Suarez?
    Che Guevara?
    Fidel Castro?

WHERE NEXT?

Brazil, Paraguay, Argentina, Chile or Peru.

Botswana

1. **Until its independence in 1966, what was Botswana called?**
   Northern Rhodesia?
   Tanganyika?
   South West Africa?
   Bechuanaland?

2. **The Bawangwato tribal chief, who had an English wife, was elected President of Botswana in 1966. What was his name?**
   Kenneth Kaunda?
   Milton Obote?
   Noel Odingar?
   Seretse Khama?

3. **The discovery of what resource made a significant impact on the Botswana economy in 1969?**
   Oil?
   Tin?
   Natural gas?
   Diamonds?

WHERE NEXT?

Angola, Zambia, Zimbabwe or South Africa.

Brazil

1. Oscar Niemayer and Lucio Costa headed the team that designed Brazil's modern capital. What is it called?
    Sao Paulo?
    Rio de Janeiro?
    Costa Niemayer?
    Brasilia?

2. Brazil is the world's largest exporter of what product?
    Bananas?
    Maize?
    Coffee?
    Rice?

3. Brazil has a population in excess of 100,000,000 and covers an area in excess of 3,000,000 square miles. The Amazon river is in Brazil. In size how does it compare with the other great rivers of the world? Is it:
    The world's longest river?
    The second longest?
    The third longest?
    The fourth longest?

WHERE NEXT?

Venezuela, Colombia, Peru, Bolivia, Paraguay or Uruguay.

Brunei

1. **The coast of Brunei is washed by which sea?**
   The Indian Ocean?
   The Red Sea?
   The Mediterranean?
   The South China Sea?

2. **What is the title of Brunei's Head of State?**
   President?
   King?
   Sultan?
   Sheikh?

3. **Which country is responsible for the foreign affairs and defence of Brunei?**
   Brunei itself?
   The United States?
   The United Kingdom?
   Malaysia?

WHERE NEXT?

Malaysia or Indonesia.

Bulgaria

1. **What was the name of the Treaty, signed in 1878, that carved Bulgaria out of the Ottoman Empire?**
   The Treaty of Rome?
   The Treaty of Versailles?
   The Treaty of Vienna?
   The Treaty of Berlin?

2. **What happened to the Bulgarian monarchy in 1946? Was it:**
   Abolished by referendum?
   Restored after six years of Presidential rule?
   Abruptly ended when Communist troops stormed the royal palace in Sofia and murdered the royal family?
   Transformed into a constitutional monarchy?

3. **The Bulgarians share an alphabet with the Russians. What is it called?**
   Arabic?
   Roman?
   Cyrillic?
   Greek?

WHERE NEXT?

Yugoslavia, Rumania, Turkey or Greece.

Burma

1. **Between 1961 and 1971 a Burmese was Secretary General of the United Nations. What was his name?**
   Trigve Lie?
   Dag Hammarskjold?
   U Thant?
   David Ben Gurion?

2. **What is the principal feature of the weather in Burma from June to October each year?**
   The drought?
   The monsoons?
   Electrical storms?
   Dry tropical heat?

3. **What is the capital of Burma?**
   Rangoon?
   Mandalay?
   Moulmein?
   Bassein?

WHERE NEXT?

Bangladesh, India, China, Laos or Thailand.

Burundi

1. Burundi was once part of Ruanda-Urundi. In 1914 Ruanda-Urundi was a German possession. In that year, which country took Ruanda-Urundi from Germany?
    The United Kingdom?
    Spain?
    France?
    Belgium?

2. Bujumbura is the capital of Burundi and its main port. What is the name of the water that makes the port possible?
    The Atlantic Ocean?
    The Indian Ocean?
    Lake Tanganyika?
    Lake Victoria?

3. The Tutsis were the tribe that traditionally ruled the country. Although in the minority they were served by the majority of the Hutu tribe. What is the special feature of the Tutsis? Are they:
    Pygmies?
    Half-castes?
    Very tall?
    Red-headed?

WHERE NEXT?

Zaïre, Rwanda or Tanzania.

Cameroon

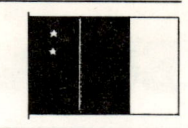

1. **During the First World War the German colony of Kamerun was occupied by two other European countries. What were they?**
   Belgium and the Netherlands?
   Spain and Portugal?
   Italy and Japan?
   France and Britain?

2. **The Cameroon Mountains are an isolated group of volcanic mountains (last known to erupt in 1922) of which the Great Cameroon is the tallest mountain in West Africa. How high is it?**
   8,000 ft?
   13,350 ft?
   19,000 ft?
   43,350 ft?

3. **Onto what water does the south-west coast of Cameroon open?**
   The Atlantic Ocean?
   The Gulf of Guinea?
   The Caribbean?
   The Irish Sea?

WHERE NEXT?

Nigeria, Chad, Central African Empire, Congo, Gabon or Equatorial Guinea.

Canada

1. In what year did the maple-leaf flag replace the red ensign as Canada's national flag?
    1906?
    1948?
    1964?
    1970?

2. What percentage of the Canadian population is reckoned to be French-speaking?
    3%
    11%
    19%
    30%

3. From 1935 to 1956 Canada had successive Liberal governments. In 1957 the country had a new Conservative government. Who was its Prime Minister?
    John Diefenbaker?
    Lester Pearson?
    Pierre Trudeau?
    Robert Menzies?

WHERE NEXT?

The United States.

Canary Islands

1. The Canary Islands are an archipelago in the Atlantic off the African coast, consisting of seven islands and six uninhabited islets. The Canaries form two provinces of which European country?
    Spain?
    Portugal?
    Italy?
    Denmark?

2. According to the poet Pliny, how did the islands get their name? Was it because:
    The sand on the beaches was canary yellow?
    The islands were full of canaries?
    The islands were full of dogs?
    The islands were named after the Greek playwright Canaricles?

3. Which is the largest city in the Canary Islands?
    Las Palmas?
    Santa Cruz de Tenerife?
    Lanzarote?
    Gomera?

WHERE NEXT?

Morocco, Mauritania, or Western Sahara.

Cape Verde Islands

1. **Where would you find the Cape Verde Islands?**
   Off the West Coast of India?
   Off the West Coast of Africa?
   Off the West Coast of the United States?
   Off the East Coast of Brazil?

2. **What is the present government of the islands?**
   An independent republic within the Commonwealth?
   A Portuguese colony?
   A Communist republic?
   A constitutional monarchy?

3. **The islands are of military importance to which major power?**
   The United States?
   The Soviet Union?
   France?
   The United Kingdom?

WHERE NEXT?

Western Sahara, Mauritania, Senegal, Gambia or Guinea Bissau.

Central African Empire

1. **The Central African Empire gained its independence in 1960. In 1966 its constitution was suspended 'indefinitely' by the President who established a military dictatorship of his own. What was his name?**
    General Amin?
    General Alexander?
    General Bokassa?
    General Dacko?

2. **Two rivers form the northern and southern boundaries of the country and until independence they gave the country its name. What are the rivers called?**
    Ubangi and Shari?
    Docki and Huto?
    Obingo and Chadra?
    Tiago and Fogo?

3. **In 1977 what did the military dictator of the Central African Republic do?**
    Execute every member of the Zande tribe?
    Sign a non-aggression pact with the Soviet Union?
    Abolish the death penalty?
    Crown himself Emperor in the manner of Napoleon?

WHERE NEXT?

Cameroon, Chad, Sudan, Zaïre or Congo.

Chad

1. In April 1975 Chad became the nineteenth military dictatorship in Africa when President Tombalbaye was murdered and the army seized power. Who led the military take-over?
    General Odingar?
    General Nkrumah?
    General Bokassa?
    General Biafra?

2. What are the mountains that you will find to the north of Chad?
    The Chad Mountains?
    The Sahara Mountains?
    The North African Alps?
    The Libyan Peaks?

3. What is the capital of Chad?
    Fort Lamy?
    Bangui?
    Rabat?
    N'Djamene?

WHERE NEXT?

Cameroon, Nigeria, Niger, Libya, Sudan or Central African Empire.

Chile

1. **What was the name of the Marxist President of Chile who was overthrown in September 1973 and killed himself when his palace was besieged?**
   Peron?
   Frei?
   Guevara?
   Allende?

2. **Chile is a long, narrow strip of territory. How long?**
   Over 1,000 miles?
   Over 1,800 miles?
   Over 2,600 miles?
   Over 8,000 miles?

3. **What is unique about Chile's Atacama Desert? Is it:**
   A United States rocket-launch base?
   The lowest point on earth?
   The world's largest desert?
   The world's driest place where rain has never been recorded?

WHERE NEXT?

Peru, Bolivia or Argentina.

China

1. When was the Manchu dynasty in China overthrown?
    1750?
    1911?
    1945?
    1959?

2. China is the world's most populous country. Roughly how many people are there in China?
    500,000,000?
    900,000,000?
    20,000,000,000?
    31,000,000,000?

3. Tourists at Peking can visit the beautiful Winter Palace. By whom was it built?
    Ghenghis Khan?
    Kubla Khan?
    Mao Tse Tung?
    Chiang Kai-shek?

WHERE NEXT?

Vietnam, Laos, Burma, Bhutan, Nepal, the Soviet Union, North Korea or South Korea.

Colombia

1. **Who founded Greater Colombia in 1819?**
    Walter Scott?
    Henry Livingstone?
    Simon Bolivar?
    Cecil Rhodes?

2. **Bogota, the capital of modern Colombia, is famous for the architecture of which great twentieth-century architect?**
    Le Corbusier?
    Van de Rohe?
    Frank Lloyd Wright?
    Basil Spence?

3. **What currency is used in Colombia?**
    The Colombian dollar?
    The Colombian pound?
    The peso?
    The franc?

WHERE NEXT?

Panama, Venezuela, Brazil, Peru or Ecuador.

Congo

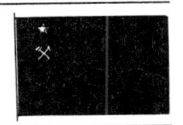

1. The People's Republic of the Congo has another name. It is also the name of the country's capital. What is it?
    Youlu?
    Kinshasa?
    Brazzaville?
    Makoua?

2. In 1975 the Congo became the base for Soviet and Cuban intervention into which other African state?
    Zaïre?
    Angola?
    Gabon?
    Central African Republic?

3. Until its independence in 1960 how was the Congo known? Was it as:
    Belgian Congo?
    Bakongo?
    Middle Congo?
    French Congo?

WHERE NEXT?

Gabon, Cameroon, Central African Empire, Zaïre or Angola.

Costa Rica

1. **What is the governmental system of Costa Rica?**
    The 50th State of the United States?
    A Presidential democracy?
    A constitutional monarchy?
    A communist military dictatorship?

2. **From an economic standpoint, what's special about Costa Rica? Is it:**
    The poorest country in Latin America?
    The country with the highest income *per capita* in Latin America?
    The country which receives more foreign aid for its size than any other in the world?
    The only country in the world where bartering is still more widely used than currency?

3. **What is the capital of Costa Rica?**
    San Sebastian?
    San José?
    Lima?
    Limon?

WHERE NEXT?

Nicaragua or Panama.

Cuba

1. Discovered by Columbus in 1492, it was settled by the Spanish by 1511. When did the United States take Cuba from Spain?
    1776?
    1815?
    1898?
    1942?

2. What was the name of the Cuban leader who came to power in 1933, with United States backing, and was deposed by Fidel Castro in 1959?
    Gracia?
    Batista?
    Allende?
    Havana?

3. In which year was there a confrontation between the United States and the Soviet Union when the Russians attempted to set up a missile base on Cuba?
    1955?
    1959?
    1962?
    1967?

WHERE NEXT?

United States, Bahamas, Haiti or Jamaica.

Cyprus

1. **Who was President of Cyprus from 1960 until his death in 1977?**
    Glafcos Clerides?
    Colonel Grivas?
    Archbishop Makarios?
    Dom Mintoff?

2. **Ninety-six per cent of the population of Cyprus are of Greek or Turkish origin. What percentage are of Greek origin?**
    17%?
    25%?
    40%?
    78%?

3. **The Greek for Cyprus is Kypros and the word Kypros gives a clue to the product for which Cyprus was famous in days of antiquity. What was it?**
    Kippers?
    Gold?
    Jade?
    Copper?

WHERE NEXT?

Turkey, Syria or Lebanon.

Czechoslovakia

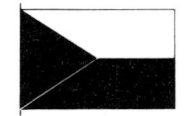

1. In 1918 Czechoslovakia was formed from three countries. Slovakia was one of the three. What were the other two?
    Albania and Austria?
    Silvania and Ruritania?
    Bohemia and Moravia?
    Poland and the Ukraine?

2. In what year did the Soviet Union invade Czechoslovakia?
    1948?
    1958?
    1968?
    1978?

3. What was the name of the liberalising Party Secretary whom the Soviet Union replaced after the invasion of Czechoslovakia?
    Husak?
    Masaryk?
    Svoboda?
    Dubček?

WHERE NEXT?

Hungary, Austria, East Germany, West Germany or Poland.

Denmark

1. **In January 1972 King Frederik IX of Denmark died. Who followed him onto the Danish throne?**
    Frederik X?
    Margrethe II?
    Beatrix?
    Carl-Gustaf IV?

2. **Denmark's most famous writer was Hans Christian Andersen (1805–1875). In 1952 a musical film was made of his life and work. Who starred in the film?**
    Tommy Steele?
    Frank Sinatra?
    Danny Kaye?
    Gene Kelly?

3. **When did Denmark join the European Economic Community?**
    1957?
    1964?
    1972?
    Never?

WHERE NEXT?

Norway, Sweden, West Germany or East Germany.

Dominican Republic

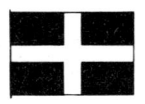

1. The Dominican Republic has shared the island of Hispaniola with another country since 1844. What is the other country?
    Haiti?
    Cuba?
    Honduras?
    Jamaica?

2. The man elected President of the Dominican Republic in 1930 was its dictator until his assassination in 1961. What was his name?
    Rafael Trujillo?
    Joaquin Balaguer?
    Juan Bosch?
    Jaime Fernandez?

3. What is the capital of the Dominican Republic?
    Santo Domingo?
    Santiago?
    La Vega?
    San Cristobal?

WHERE NEXT?

Haiti, Jamaica, Cuba or the Bahamas.

East Germany

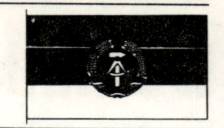

1. **What is the correct description of East Germany?**
    The German Federal Republic?
    The German Democratic Republic?
    The Socialist Republic of Eastern Germany?
    The United German Republic?

2. **How many refugees have succeeded in leaving East Germany since 1945?**
    Over 6,000?
    Over 670,000?
    Over 1,000,000?
    Over 3,600,000?

3. **In which year was the Berlin Wall erected?**
    1945?
    1948?
    1957?
    1961?

WHERE NEXT?

Poland, Czechoslovakia, West Germany.

Ecuador

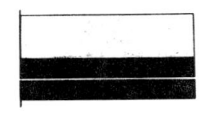

1. To my great shame, in the *Pears Family Quiz Book* I gave Bogota as the capital of Ecuador! As scores of readers were quick to point out: Bogota is the capital of Colombia. What then *is* the capital of Ecuador?
    Caracas?
    Lima?
    Quito?
    La Paz?

2. Fifty per cent of all Ecuador's exports are of one product. They are the world's largest exporters of this commodity and have captured a quarter of the world market. What is the product?
    Zinc?
    Balsa wood?
    Cocoa?
    Bananas?

3. What is the name of the Ecuador currency?
    The sucre?
    The escudo?
    The Ecu-dollar?
    The peso?

WHERE NEXT?

Colombia or Peru.

Egypt

1. **Cleopatra was Queen of Egypt a long time ago. When exactly did she die?**
   300 B.C.?
   30 B.C.?
   A.D. 300?
   A.D. 1300?

2. **The last King of Egypt was forced to abdicate in 1952. What was his name?**
   Aly Khan?
   Hussein?
   Farouk?
   Ptolemy?

3. **Colonel Nasser became President of Egypt in 1954. What happened to him in September 1970? Did he:**
   Resign as a result of the Six-Day War with Israel?
   Get murdered by a group of Palestinian extremists?
   Hand over power voluntarily to Anwar Sadat?
   Die of a heart attack?

WHERE NEXT?

Libya, Sudan, Israel, Jordan or Saudi Arabia.

El Salvador

1. **What is the capital of El Salvador?**
   El Salvador?
   Tia Salvador?
   Con Salvador?
   San Salvador?

2. **El Salvador is a member of O.C.A.S. What do the initials stand for?**
   Organisation of Central American States?
   Organisation of Coffee and Sugar Exporting Countries?
   Organisation of Communist Americans of the South?
   Official Congress of American States?

3. **Volcanos and earthquakes are a feature of El Salvador. In 1965 the capital was severely damaged by earthquakes. Cotopaxi is the name of the world's highest active volcano. In which country would you find it?**
   El Salvador?
   Ecuador?
   Mexico?
   Guatemala?

WHERE NEXT?

Guatemala, Honduras or Nicaragua.

Equatorial Guinea

1. **Equatorial Guinea is a country in two parts. One part is a small area of land between Cameroon and Gabon called Rio Muni. What is the other part?**
    A small area of land inside Nigeria?
    A rock with nothing but a lighthouse on it in the Gulf of Guinea?
    A volcanic island called Sao Mao?
    A number of islands, the main one being Fernando Poo?

2. **Until independence Equatorial Guinea was a certain European country's only African territory south of the Sahara. What was that country?**
    Spain?
    Belgium?
    Germany?
    France?

3. **What is the capital of Equatorial Guinea?**
    Santa Isabel?
    Santa Sebastiane?
    Santa Cruz?
    Malabo?

WHERE NEXT?

Nigeria, Cameroon or Gabon.

Ethiopia

1. **Ethiopia is the oldest independent state in Africa. Traditionally, the founder of the Ethiopian royal line in about 1000 B.C. was Menelik. Who were his parents?**
    Antony and Cleopatra?
    Solomon and the Queen of Sheba?
    Rameses III and Volumnia?
    Pyramus and Thisbe?

2. **Haile Selassie was crowned 225th ruler of Ethiopia in 1930. What was the title he gave himself as well as that of Emperor?**
    'The King of Kings'?
    'The Lord of the Jungle'?
    'The Lion of Judah'?
    'The Son of Menelik'?

3. **A former Italian colony was federated to Ethiopia in 1952 and was integrated into Ethiopia in 1962. What was the colony called?**
    Eritrea?
    Asmara?
    Diredawa?
    Dessie?

WHERE NEXT?

Somali Democratic Republic, Kenya or Sudan.

Fiji

1. **Fiji consists of how many islands?**
    1?
    8?
    72?
    322?

2. **Fiji was discovered by a famous explorer in 1642. Who was he?**
    Christopher Columbus?
    Abel Tasman?
    Henry Livingstone?
    Amerigo Vespucci?

3. **Ethnically, only about 42 per cent of the Fijian population are Fijians. What is the origin of 50 per cent of the population?**
    Polynesian?
    European?
    Australian?
    India?

WHERE NEXT?

Tonga, American Samoa or Western Samoa.

Finland

1. **In 1809 Finland was taken by one country from another. Who took it from whom?**
   Russia took it from Sweden?
   Britain took it from the Netherlands?
   Norway took it from Bosnia?
   Sweden took it from France?

2. **What was the name of the composer who wrote *Finlandia*?**
   Puccini?
   Sibelius?
   Dvorak?
   Rimsky-Korsakov?

3. **Nine per cent of Finland's 130,160 square miles is covered by lakes. What percentage of the country is covered by forests?**
   10%?
   20%?
   30%?
   70%?

WHERE NEXT?

Soviet Union, Norway or Sweden.

France

1. **Under the Fifth French Republic, for how many years is the President elected?**
   - 4?
   - 5?
   - 7?
   - 9?

2. **Compared with the United Kingdom, how large is France?**
   - About the same size?
   - Slightly larger?
   - Slightly smaller?
   - About twice the size?

3. **Who succeeded Charles de Gaulle as President of France in 1969?**
   - Valéry Giscard d'Estaing?
   - Pierre Coty?
   - Georges Pompidou?
   - Jacques Chirac?

WHERE NEXT?

Belgium, Luxembourg, West Germany, Switzerland, Italy, Monaco, Spain or Andorra.

French Guiana

1. Until the last convicts returned to France in 1945, French Guiana was used mainly as a penal settlement. What part of the country was most famous as a penal stronghold?
    Alcatraz?
    Devil's Island?
    St Helena?
    Port Prisonnier?

2. Between which two South American states is French Guiana situated?
    Venezuela and Guyana?
    Surinam and Brazil?
    Bolivia and Paraguay?
    Argentina and Uruguay?

3. What is the capital of French Guiana?
    Bienvenue?
    Saint George?
    Port Albert?
    Cayenne?

WHERE NEXT?

Surinam or Brazil.

French Polynesia

1. **How many islands are there in French Polynesia?**
    - 6?
    - 76?
    - 156?
    - 1,006?

2. **The capital is Papeete. On which of the islands is it?**
    - Bali?
    - Samoa?
    - Tonga?
    - Tahiti?

3. **A French painter who lived from 1848 to 1903 dearly loved the islands of French Polynesia and painted there. What was his name?**
    - François Millet?
    - Paul Gauguin?
    - Edgar Degas?
    - Paul Cézanne?

WHERE NEXT?

New Zealand.

Gabon

1. Who ran a hospital leper colony at Lambaréné in Gabon from 1913 until his death in 1965?
    Blaise Pascal?
    Trevor Huddleston?
    Jacques Tati?
    Albert Schweitzer?

2. What has the name of the President of Gabon been since 1967?
    Bingo?
    Bongo?
    Bungo?
    Bango?

3. Gabon covers an area of over 100,000 miles. How many men are in the Gabon armed forces?
    960?
    8,600?
    20,500?
    110,000?

WHERE NEXT?

Equatorial Guinea, Cameroon, Congo or Angola.

Gambia

1. **What is the capital of the Gambia?**
    Chichester?
    Banjul?
    Washington?
    Jolas?

2. **The Gambia's first elections were held in 1966. Who won them and has been President since?**
    Sir Dawda Jawara?
    Sir Ruby Sithole?
    Chief Rama Brunganinbe?
    Chief Kao?

3. **The Gambia covers an area of 4,000 square miles. What is the country's population?**
    About 500,000?
    About 1,000,000?
    About 5,000,000?
    About 15,000,000?

WHERE NEXT?

Senegal or Guinea Bissau.

Ghana

1. **Before independence, what was Ghana called?**
    The Belgian Congo?
    The Ivory Coast?
    The Gold Coast?
    British Guinea?

2. **He called himself 'the Redeemer', became Premier when the country achieved independence in 1957 and President when it became a Republic in 1960. He was overthrown in 1966. What was his name?**
    Julius Nyere?
    Kenneth Kaunda?
    Albert Djibouti?
    Kwame Nkrumah?

3. **The largest man-made harbour in Africa is in Ghana. What is it called?**
    Accra Harbour?
    Tema Harbour?
    Kumasi Harbour?
    Volta Harbour?

WHERE NEXT?

Ivory Coast, Voltaic Republic or Togo.

Gibraltar

1. **What was Gibraltar called in the times of the ancient Greeks and Romans?**
   The Rock?
   The Point?
   The Calpe?
   The Bunion?

2. **In the referendum held in 1967, 12,138 of the people of Gibraltar voted in favour of retaining the link with Britain and against uniting with Spain. How many voted against Britain and for Spain?**
   44?
   1,009?
   8,600?
   11,983?

3. **To what height does the famous Rock of Gibraltar rise?**
   871 ft?
   1,396 ft?
   12,000 ft?
   Not at all: the 'Rock' is merely an expression used to describe the promontory, which has no significant height?

WHERE NEXT?

Spain or Morocco.

Gilbert Islands

1. The Gilbert Islands are a chain of coral islands in the central Pacific Ocean. Though still a British crown colony, the Ellice Islands separated from the Gilbert Islands in 1976 and were renamed. What is the Ellice Islands' new name?
    Sullivan?
    Tuvalu?
    Tatta?
    Bairiki?

2. One of the most famous of the islands in the group was discovered by Captain Cook in 1777. It is the world's largest atoll. What's it called?
    Cook Island?
    Fiji?
    Christmas Island?
    The Isle of Dogs?

3. Britain provides the islands with protection. So does another country. Which is it?
    New Guinea?
    New Caledonia?
    New Zealand?
    Australia?

WHERE NEXT?

Papua New Guinea, Solomon Islands, Fiji or Australia.

Greece

1. **To which part of Greece would you go to find the Temple of Apollo and Mount Parnassus?**
    Athens?
    Thebes?
    Delphi?
    Corfu?

2. **King Constantine of Greece was born in 1940. He came to the throne in 1964. In what year was he forced to flee his country and to where did he first go?**
    Rome in 1967?
    London in 1969?
    Paris in 1971?
    Peru in 1973?

3. **Who wrote the music for the film *Zorba the Greek*?**
    Michael Cacoyannis?
    Constatine Karamanlis?
    Mikis Theodorakis?
    Anthony Quinn?

WHERE NEXT?

Albania, Yugoslavia, Bulgaria or Turkey.

Grenada

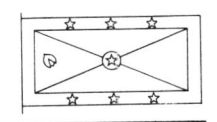

1. **Grenada is the most southerly of which famous group of islands in the West Indies?**
   The Windward Islands?
   The Leeward Islands?
   The Emerald Islands?
   The Nutmeg Islands?

2. **Christopher Columbus discovered Grenada in 1498. Where was Columbus born?**
   Florence?
   Genoa?
   Southend?
   Amsterdam?

3. **When 'Miss Grenada' won the Miss World beauty contest, one of the judges was Grenada's Prime Minister. What was his name?**
   Eric Morley?
   Eric Morecambe?
   Eric Marriott?
   Eric Gairy?

WHERE NEXT?

Barbados, Guadeloupe, Trinidad and Tobago or Venezuela.

Guadeloupe

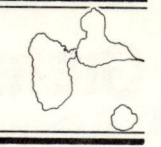

1. **With its dependent islands, Guadeloupe has rather a special international status. What is it?**
    A neutral zone administered by the U.N.?
    The oldest monarchy in the Caribbean?
    A republic within the British Commonwealth?
    A Department of France?

2. **Guadeloupe was discovered by Christopher Columbus in 1493. After what was it named?**
    Columbus's mother-in-law, Francesca Guadeloupe?
    The Guadeloupe melon found on the island?
    The first officer on board Columbus's ship?
    A monastery in Spain?

3. **Many of the settlers of Guadeloupe were Normans and Bretons. During the French Revolution what action did they take?**
    Oppose the Revolution?
    Guillotine their plantation owners?
    Briefly rename the islands 'Robespierre'?
    None at all?

WHERE NEXT?

Barbados, Grenada, or Trinidad and Tobago.

Guam

1. **Who is Guam's Head of State?**
   President Rudolph Bordallo?
   King Ricardo III?
   Queen Elizabeth II?
   The President of the United States?

2. **What is the capital of Guam?**
   Agana?
   Havana?
   Guyana?
   Upi?

3. **The Portuguese navigator, Ferdinand Magellan, is believed to have discovered Guam in 1521, the year of his death. For what seafaring 'first' is Magellan famous? Was he:**
   The first navigator to sail round the world?
   The first navigator to use a compass?
   The first navigator to keep his crew's provisions in salt?
   The first navigator to sail south of the Equator?

WHERE NEXT?

Papua New Guinea, Philippines, Taiwan or Japan.

Guatemala

1. **Guatemala is the world's second largest producer of chicle. In what familiar product is chicle used?**
    Washing-up liquid?
    Blotting paper?
    Rat poison?
    Chewing gum?

2. **In pre-Columbian times Guatemala was the centre of which famous civilisation?**
    The Mayan civilisation?
    The Ancient Greek civilisation?
    The Aztec civilisation?
    The Montenegrine civilisation?

3. **Guatemala City is the country's capital. It was founded in 1776 to replace the former capital of Antigua. Why?**
    Because Antigua was:
    over-run with the plague?
    destroyed by earthquakes?
    destroyed by Mexican bandits?
    given to the United States of America as an Independence gift?

WHERE NEXT?

Mexico, Belize, Honduras or El Salvador.

Guinea

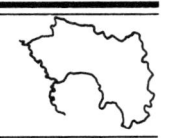

1. **What does the Guinea flag look like? Is it:**
    A guinea pig on an azure background?
    A hammer and sickle on a pink background?
    Three vertical stripes of red, yellow and green?
    Five gold stars on a turquoise background?

2. **In 1958 Guinea became the only French colony to take a certain action. What did it do?**
    Choose independence outside the French Community?
    Refuse to take part in the referendum on the future of the French colonies?
    Vote 100 per cent in favour of the election of General de Gaulle as President?
    Accept the status of a French Department?

3. **What is the capital of Guinea?**
    Conakry?
    Toure?
    Kindia?
    Marseilles-sur-Guinea?

WHERE NEXT?

Guinea-Bissau, Senegal, Mali, Ivory Coast, Liberia or Sierra Leone.

Guinea-Bissau

1. **Of all the European colonies in Africa, what was special about Guinea-Bissau? Was it:**
    The oldest European colony in Africa?
    The most recent European colony in Africa?
    The only colony where the whites outnumbered the blacks?
    The first colony to achieve independence in 1897?

2. **What was Guinea-Bissau called before independence?**
    Portuguese West Africa?
    Portuguese Guinea?
    French Somaliland?
    French Equatorial Africa?

3. **What was the name of the Governor of Guinea-Bissau between 1969 and 1973? He became President of Portugal in 1974.**
    General Gomez?
    General Dayan?
    General Spinola?
    General Spinoza?

WHERE NEXT?

Senegal or Guinea.

Guyana

1. For many years Guyana was claimed by another South American country. The claim was dropped in 1970 when Guyana became independent. What was the country that had claimed Guyana?
    Surinam?
    Brazil?
    Venezuela?
    Chile?

2. What is the capital of Guyana?
    Jamestown?
    Georgetown?
    Freetown?
    Downtown?

3. What industry has always been the mainstay of the Guyana economy?
    Tourism?
    Cotton wool?
    Sugar?
    Groundnuts?

WHERE NEXT?

Venezuela, Brazil or Surinam.

Haiti

1. **What was the title of Graham Greene's novel about Haiti?**
    The Power and the Glory?
    The Great Dictator?
    This Island Story?
    The Comedians?

2. **From 1957 until his death in 1971 the dictator of Haiti was the President, known to all as 'Papa Doc'. What was his real name?**
    Maurice Chevalier?
    François Duvalier?
    Jean-Pierre Cassoulet?
    Docteur Knock?

3. **When Papa Doc died, who succeeded him as President for Life?**
    His son, Jean-Claude, known as 'Baby Doc'?
    His grandson, André, known as 'Dodo Doc'?
    His wife, Marie-Claude, known as 'Mama Doc'?
    Robert Houdin, the Prime Minister?

WHERE NEXT?

Dominican Republic, Cuba, Bahamas or Jamaica.

Honduras

1. **In round numbers, how many revolutions and *coups d'état* has Honduras known since independence from Spain in 1838?**
    Over 10?
    Over 50?
    Over 100?
    Over 1,000?

2. **What happened on the north coast of Honduras in 1974? Was it:**
    The site for the 1974 Olympic Games?
    Devastated by Hurricane Fifi?
    The site of the largest discovery of oil in South America?
    Destroyed by the eruption of the Titicanoo Volcano?

3. **In Copan in Honduras there are ruins to be seen that date back to the Mayan civilisation. Roughly how far back do the ruins date?**
    4th–8th centuries?
    8th–12th centuries?
    12th–16th centuries?
    16th–18th centuries?

WHERE NEXT?

Belize, Guatemala, El Salvador or Nicaragua.

Hong Kong

1. **What is the status of Hong Kong? Is it:**
    A British colony?
    An independent republic within the Commonwealth?
    An independent monarchy within the Commonwealth?
    A Cinque Port within the Commonwealth?

2. **What is the capital of Hong Kong?**
    Hong Kong?
    Kowloon?
    Victoria?
    Aberdeen?

3. **Britain seized Hong Kong from China in 1841. In 1898 Britain leased the 'New Territories' from China. When is the lease on the New Territories due to expire?**
    1984?
    1997?
    2098?
    2898?

WHERE NEXT?

China, Taiwan or Vietnam.

Hungary

1. **Who set up the first Communist Republic in Hungary and when?**
   Bela Kun in 1919?
   Leon Trotsky in 1929?
   Matyas Rakosi in 1939?
   The Soviet Union in 1946?

2. **What was the name of the Hungarian Prime Minister who, between 1953 and 1956, attempted to introduce liberalising reforms?**
   Nagy?
   Kadar?
   Fock?
   Dubček?

3. **Hungarians speak Hungarian. What is the other, older name for their language?**
   Serbo-Croat?
   Magyar?
   Pecs?
   Austro-Hungarian?

WHERE NEXT?

Yugoslavia, Austria, Czechoslovakia, Soviet Union or Rumania.

Iceland

1. **From which country did Iceland gain its independence in 1944?**
   Greenland?
   Norway?
   Finland?
   Denmark?

2. **The 'cod war' of 1975 came about because Iceland wanted to extend the limit of her territorial waters. To what distance did she want to extend them?**
   50 miles?
   100 miles?
   200 miles?
   500 miles?

3. **What is the size of the combined Icelandic army and air force?**
   80,000 men?
   8,000 men?
   800 men?
   No men at all, because Iceland has neither an army nor an air force?

WHERE NEXT?

Norway or United Kingdom.

India

1. What percentage of the Indian population is Hindu?
    12%?
    29%?
    64%?
    84%?

2. Which Indian city is the site of the 'seven ancient cities' of India?
    Delhi?
    Bombay?
    Calcutta?
    Madras?

3. For a decade, beginning in 1966, Mrs Gandhi was India's Prime Minister. Who was Prime Minister before her?
    Mahatma Gandhi?
    Nehru?
    Shastri?
    Sharma?

WHERE NEXT?

Pakistan, Nepal, Sri Lanka or Bangladesh.

Indonesia

1. **On which of the islands of Indonesia will you find the capital of Djakarta?**
    Sumatra?
    Java?
    Madura?
    Sulawesi?

2. **Who led Indonesia to independence in 1949 and became its first President?**
    Sukarno?
    Suharto?
    Harahap?
    Malik?

3. **In what part of Indonesia does the tourist find the last Hindu civilisation in South-East Asia?**
    Bali?
    Timor?
    Padang?
    Menado?

WHERE NEXT?

Malaysia, Singapore, Philippines or Australia.

Iran

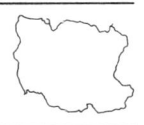

1. **What is the principal language of Iran?**
   English?
   Teheranese?
   Tomates?
   Farsi?

2. **The present Shah of Iran succeeded his father who abdicated. In what year was that?**
   1941?
   1951?
   1959?
   1967?

3. **What was the name of the famous Persian astronomer-poet who died in 1122?**
   Ali Baba?
   Omar Khayyam?
   Abu ben Ali?
   Shah Kurd?

WHERE NEXT?

Pakistan, Afghanistan, Soviet Union, Iraq, Kuwait or Saudi Arabia.

Iraq

1. **The remains of which of the Seven Wonders of the World will you find in Iraq?**
    The Tomb of Mausolus?
    The Pharos of Alexandria?
    The Hanging Gardens of Babylon?
    The Statue of Jupiter at Olympus?

2. **What happened to King Faisal II of Iraq in 1958? Was he:**
    Forced to abdicate?
    Assassinated?
    Killed in an aeroplane accident?
    Made President for Life when the country became a republic?

3. **Of what commodity is Iraq the world's largest producer, supplying 80 per cent of the world market?**
    Tobacco?
    Linseed oil?
    Rice?
    Dates?

WHERE NEXT?

Syria, Turkey, Iran, Kuwait or Saudi Arabia.

Ireland

1. **When did the Dublin Parliament declare the Irish Free State?**
    1919?
    1922?
    1926?
    1935?

2. **In 1937 Southern Ireland was renamed. What was the country's new name?**
    Gaella?
    Eire?
    Free Ireland?
    Ulster?

3. **During the Second World War what was Ireland's position?**
    One of the Allies?
    Pro-German?
    A member of a special British-American alliance?
    Neutral?

WHERE NEXT?

United Kingdom or Iceland.

Israel

1. **Until the Six-Day War of 1967 Jerusalem was controlled by two countries. Israel was one. What was the other?**
    Syria?
    Jordan?
    Iraq?
    Egypt?

2. **What was the name of Israel's Prime Minister during the Six-Day War?**
    Golda Meir?
    Levi Eshkol?
    Moshe Dayan?
    Yitzhak Rabin?

3. **In 1976 the Israelis rescued over a hundred hijacked hostages from an airport in which foreign country?**
    West Germany?
    Zaïre?
    Uganda?
    Saudi Arabia?

WHERE NEXT?

Egypt, Saudi Arabia, Jordan, Syria or Lebanon.

Italy

1. In May 1978 a former Prime Minister of Italy was murdered by his kidnappers. What was his name?
    Giovanni Leone?
    Giulio Andreotti?
    Aldo Moro?
    Franco Malfatti?

2. In which Italian city will you find the Doges' Palace, San Marco and the Rialto Bridge?
    Venice?
    Florence?
    Padua?
    Rome?

3. Italy is the world's largest producer of which product?
    Motor cars?
    Wine?
    Machine tools?
    Olive oil?

WHERE NEXT?

France, Switzerland, Austria, Yugoslavia or Tunisia, Vatican City or San Marino.

Ivory Coast

1. **What is the capital of the Ivory Coast?**
   Abidjan?
   Daloa?
   Accra?
   Libreville?

2. **Who was elected President of the Ivory Coast in 1960, 1965, 1970 and 1975?**
   Felix Houphouet-Boigny?
   Jaspar Kinky-Boissy?
   Charles Kolobouake?
   Ali Bongo?

3. **How does the government of the Ivory Coast differ from other black African governments in its attitude to South Africa? Does it want to:**
   Invade South Africa?
   Establish a dialogue and détente with South Africa?
   Introduce apartheid to the Ivory Coast?
   Amalgamate with South Africa?

WHERE NEXT?

Liberia, Guinea, Mali, Voltaic Republic or Ghana.

Jamaica

1. Jamaica was discovered by Columbus in 1494 and occupied by the Spanish from 1509 until 1655 when the British captured the island. Who ordered the expedition?
    Charles II?
    Oliver Cromwell?
    Samuel Pepys?
    No one in particular. Admiral Penn and his fleet were passing the island and decided to capture it of their own initiative?

2. What is the name of the famous range of mountains in Jamaica?
    The Blue Mountains?
    The Black Mountains?
    The Kingston Mountains?
    The Montego Mountains?

3. Who is Jamaica's Head of State?
    Michael Manley?
    Clifford Campbell?
    Eric Bazzazzwe?
    Queen Elizabeth II?

WHERE NEXT?

Cuba, Haiti, Dominican Republic, Bahamas, Belize or Honduras.

Japan

1. **When did Emperor Hirohito renounce his divine powers?**
   - In 1947 when Japan had a new constitution?
   - In 1960 on the 1000th anniversary of the Japanese monarchy?
   - In 1975 when Queen Elizabeth II visited Japan?
   - Never. He has not renounced his divine powers.

2. **The Japanese call Japan 'Nihon Koku'. What does Nihon Koku mean?**
   - The Land of the Rising Sun?
   - The Land of the Curly Monkey?
   - The Land of the Rising Yen?
   - Ancient Land of the East?

3. **Tokyo is the present capital of Japan. The country's former capital contains the Gosho Palace, the Nijo Palace and the Golden Pavilion. What is the old capital called?**
   - Osaka?
   - Nagoya?
   - Kyoto?
   - Fukuoka?

WHERE NEXT?

North Korea, South Korea, China, Taiwan or Soviet Union.

Jordan

1. **How old was King Hussein when he succeeded King Talal in 1952?**
   Six?
   Seventeen?
   Twenty-three?
   Thirty?

2. **In May 1978 King Hussein announced that he planned to marry again. What will his new wife be?**
   His second wife?
   His third?
   His fourth?
   His seventh?

3. **Prince Hassan is the Crown Prince of Jordan. Who was his father?**
   King Hussein?
   King Hassan?
   King Talal?
   King Hing?

WHERE NEXT?

Syria, Saudi Arabia, Egypt or Israel.

Kampuchea

1. **Until 1975 what was Kampuchea called?**
   Siam?
   Laos?
   North Vietnam?
   Cambodia?

2. **Who was the country's Head of State from 1960 until he fled to China in 1970?**
   General Lou Nol?
   Ho Chi Minh?
   Prince Sihanouk?
   Son Sen Hu Nim?

3. **What is the capital of Kampuchea?**
   Kompong Cham?
   Kampot?
   Battambang?
   Phnom Penh?

WHERE NEXT?

Thailand, Laos or Vietnam.

Kenya

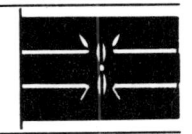

1. **What happened to President Jomo Kenyatta of Kenya in 1952? Was he:**
    Elected President for the first time?
    Made Chairman of the Organisation of African States?
    Arrested after Mau Mau attacks on white farms?
    Wounded severely in an assassination attempt?

2. **What happened to the Asian traders in Kenya in 1968? Were they:**
    All arrested and deported?
    Refused Kenyan citizenship?
    Murdered?
    Given special rights as 'Second Class Citizens of Kenya'?

3. **What is the capital of Kenya?**
    Mombasa?
    Kenyatta?
    Nairobi?
    Dakar?

WHERE NEXT?

Tanzania, Uganda, Sudan, Ethiopia or Somalia.

Kuwait

1. Between 1899 and 1961 there was a special agreement between Kuwait and which European country?
    France?
    Portugal?
    United Kingdom?
    Greece?

2. In 1961 an important source providing 5,000,000 gallons per day of a valuable fluid was discovered at Raudhatain. What was it?
    Oil?
    Liquid gas?
    Mercury?
    Water?

3. What is the capital of Kuwait?
    Magwa?
    Al Ahmadi?
    Al Jahrah?
    Kuwait?

WHERE NEXT?

Iran, Iraq or Saudi Arabia.

Laos

1. **When was the monarchy abolished in Laos?**
    1899?
    1949?
    1960?
    1975?

2. **What is the name of the Communist party that had been attempting to seize power in Laos since the 1940s and finally succeeded in 1975?**
    The M.L.P.?
    The Puvanna Phoumas?
    The Pathet Lao?
    The Mekong Reds?

3. **What is the capital of Laos?**
    Vientiane?
    Luang Prabang?
    Laos City?
    Ho Chi Minh City?

WHERE NEXT?

Vietnam, Kampuchea, Thailand, Burma or China.

Lebanon

1. **For what is the Lebanese town of Jubail, once known as Byblos, famous? Is it:**
   The place where most of the Bible is believed to have been written?
   One of the oldest continuously inhabited towns in the world?
   The site of the world's most devastating earthquake in 1879?
   The place where the first Cedars of Lebanon were planted?

2. **Which of the plays of William Shakespeare is partly set in the Lebanon?**
   Julius Caesar?
   Othello?
   As You Like It?
   Pericles, Prince of Tyre?

3. **Which Lebanese city was largely destroyed during the fighting of 1975–78?**
   Tripoli?
   Beirut?
   Zahle?
   Saida?

WHERE NEXT?

Israel or Syria.

Lesotho

1. **Before independence what was Lesotho called?**
    Central South Africa?
    Namibia?
    Basutoland?
    Natal?

2. **Who is Lesotho's Head of State?**
    Queen Elizabeth II?
    King Moshoeshoe II?
    Emperor Napoleon II?
    Chief Kwame II?

3. **Who became Prime Minister of Lesotho in 1965 and suspended the constitution after the 1970 elections?**
    Bishop Muzorewa?
    Doctor Livingstone?
    King David?
    Chief Jonathan?

WHERE NEXT?

South Africa.

Liberia

1. **What is the capital of Liberia?**
   Liberia City?
   Garraway?
   Monrovia?
   Zomba?

2. **What is Liberia's connection with world shipping? Is it that Liberia:**
   Boasts the largest port in Africa?
   Has the largest merchant marine of any African country?
   Has a policy of providing 'a flag of convenience' for ships and tankers from many countries around the world?
   Has the world's second-largest ship-building yard?

3. **Liberia was founded by the American Colonisation Society in 1822. Why?**
   As a base for American missionary work in Africa?
   As a country for freed American slaves to live in?
   As an American naval base in the Atlantic?
   As a penal colony?

WHERE NEXT?

Sierra Leone, Guinea or Ivory Coast.

Libya

1. **Who ruled Libya from 1912 to 1942?**
    The Libyans?
    The French?
    The Italians?
    The Portuguese?

2. **What was the name of the King of Libya who was deposed in a coup in 1969?**
    King Tizer?
    King Cola?
    King Idris?
    King Quash?

3. **What will you find at Zelten, Dahra and Beida in Libya?**
    The former King's summer palaces?
    The country houses of Colonel Gadhafi?
    The country's principal ports?
    The country's main oil-fields?

WHERE NEXT?

Egypt, Chad, Niger, Algeria or Tunisia.

Liechtenstein

1. **What language do they speak in Liechtenstein?**
    German?
    Swiss French?
    Austrian?
    Liechts?

2. **How large is Liechtenstein?**
    5 square miles?
    65 square miles?
    105 square miles?
    1,248 square miles?

3. **What is the name of Liechtenstein's Head of State?**
    Prince Franz Josef II?
    Prince Carl Gustav IV?
    King Joacquim III?
    The President of Switzerland?

WHERE NEXT?

West Germany, Austria, Italy or Switzerland.

Luxembourg

1. **Between 1815 and 1890 Luxembourg was part of which other European country?**
   Belgium?
   Germany?
   France?
   Netherlands?

2. **There is a flower that is one of Luxembourg's major products. What is it?**
   The tulip?
   The rose?
   The carnation?
   The iris?

3. **French is the country's 'official' language, but Luxembourg also has a language of its own, a dialect of German, with a special name. What is it?**
   Letzeburgesch?
   Liebfraumilch?
   Unterdenlinden?
   Hottentot?

WHERE NEXT?

Belgium, West Germany or France.

Madagascar

1. **When the Portuguese first came across this island in 1500, they misnamed it 'Madagascar'. What should it have been called?**
   Malagasy?
   Mogadisho?
   Comoro?
   Tahiti?

2. **Between 1885 and 1958 who ruled the island?**
   The Spanish?
   The Portuguese?
   The French?
   The South Africans?

3. **What is the capital of the Malagasy Republic?**
   Tananarive?
   Tsirinana?
   Androka?
   Koka?

WHERE NEXT?

Seychelles, Mauritius, Tanzania, Mozambique or South Africa.

Malawi

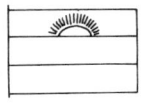

1. What was Malawi called before independence?
    Basutoland?
    French Guiana?
    Northern Rhodesia?
    Nyasaland?

2. After 43 years abroad, he returned to Malawi to win the 1961 elections, was elected President in 1966 and made himself President for Life in 1971. What is his name?
    Dr Julius Nyere?
    Dr Hastings Banda?
    Dr Milton Obote?
    Dr Kenneth Kaunda?

3. Lake Malawi is Africa's third largest lake and covers 9,270 square miles. Apart from Malawi, what countries does Lake Malawi touch?
    None?
    Mozambique and Tanzania?
    Zambia and Zaire?
    Zimbabwe?

WHERE NEXT?

Tanzania, Zambia or Mozambique.

Malaysia

1. **Malaya and Sarawak are two of the three main parts of Malaysia. What is the third?**
    Sabah?
    Borneo?
    Malacca?
    Singapore?

2. **Who is Malaysia's Supreme Head of State?**
    Tunku Abdul Rahman?
    Hussein Onn?
    Queen Elizabeth II?
    H.R.H. Tunku Yahya Putra Ibni-Marhum Sultan Ibrahim, Sultan of Kelantan?

3. **From the ninth to the fourteenth centuries Malaya was the centre of the Sri Vijaya empire. What was the Empire's religion?**
    Muslim?
    Buddhist?
    Christian?
    Taoist?

WHERE NEXT?

Indonesia, Singapore, Brunei or Philippines.

Maldive Islands

1. **How many Maldive Islands are there? And how many are inhabited?**
   Over 2,000 of which about 220 are inhabited?
   Over 1,000 of which about 110 are inhabited?
   Over 400 of which about 30 are inhabited?
   Over 50 of which 9 are inhabited?

2. **The islanders' staple diet is dried 'bonito'. What is bonito?**
   A kind of root vegetable?
   A kind of citrus fruit?
   A kind of nut?
   A kind of fish?

3. **In 1976 the R.A.F. abandoned its base on one of the islands with detrimental effects to the island's economy. What was the island called?**
   Male?
   Minicoy?
   Gan?
   Tiladummati?

WHERE NEXT?

Sri Lanka or India.

Mali

1. **Before independence what was Mali called?**
   German Nyasaland?
   French Soudan?
   Togoland?
   Dahomey?

2. **In Mali there is a small town that boasts one of the best-known names in the world. For centuries it was a centre of caravan routes and a notorious slave market, but its prosperity has declined in recent years. It has a population of 9,000. What's it called?**
   John O'Groats?
   Livingstone?
   Timbuktu?
   Olé?

3. **After eight years in office, Mali's first President, Modibo Keita, was overthrown in a *coup* in 1968. Before he became President of Mali, what did Keita do for a living? Was he:**
   A university lecturer?
   An American senator?
   An army officer?
   The leader of a dance troupe?

WHERE NEXT?

Algeria, Niger, Voltaic Republic, Ivory Coast, Guinea, Senegal or Mauritania.

Malta

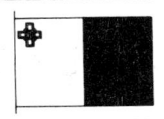

1. **Malta includes two other islands. One of them is Gozo. What is the other?**
    Bomino?
    Comino?
    Domino?
    Eomino?

2. **Who became the masters of Malta in 1530?**
    The Phoenicians?
    The Turks?
    The Greeks?
    The Knights of St John?

3. **During the Second World War some 2,000 Maltese were killed and some 35,000 Maltese homes were damaged or destroyed, but the island withstood all attacks. At the end of the war, the island was awarded an honour that it no longer uses. What was it?**
    The Victoria Cross?
    The George Cross?
    The Maltese Cross?
    The Cross of St John?

WHERE NEXT?

Italy, Greece or Tunisia.

Mauritania

1. **Until recently which other North African country claimed Mauritania?**
   Algeria?
   Western Sahara?
   Senegal?
   Morocco?

2. **Moktar Ould Daddah has been President and Prime Minister of Mauritania for almost 20 years. In the elected Assembly his party is called the Mauritanian People's Party. What is the Opposition Party called?**
   The Anti-Daddah Party?
   The People's Liberation Alliance?
   The Sahara Party?
   Nothing at all, because there is no opposition?

3. **The sovereignty of Western Sahara, formerly Spanish Sahara, was transferred from Spain to Mauritania and Morocco in 1975. What is the name of the liberation movement, backed by the Algerians, that aims at an independent Western Sahara?**
   Anti-Mauritanian Front?
   Polisario Front?
   Pan-Arab Front?
   Full Front?

WHERE NEXT?

Western Sahara, Morocco, Algeria, Mali or Senegal.

Mauritius

1. **Mauritius was discovered by the Portuguese in 1511, but it was the Dutch who gave it its name when they went there in 1598. After whom did they name the island?**
   Prince Maurice of Nassau?
   Maurice Maeterlinck?
   The Maurit flower that flourishes on the island?
   The Morris Dancers that lived on the island?

2. **Ninety per cent of the cultivated land on the island is given over to one crop. What is it?**
   Tobacco?
   Opium?
   Sweet potato?
   Sugar?

3. **What currency is used in Mauritius?**
   Mauritius dollar?
   Mauritius pound?
   Mauritius franc?
   Mauritius rupee?

WHERE NEXT?

Mozambique, Tanzania or Madagascar.

Mexico

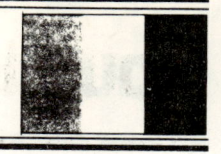

1. On the Mexican flag there are three vertical stripes of green, white and red, with an emblem in the centre. What is the emblem?
    An outline of the map of Mexico?
    A yellow rose?
    An eagle on a cactus devouring a snake?
    A palm tree?

2. 'Smoking Mountain' is the English translation of the Aztec name for the famous dormant volcano that lies about forty miles south east of Mexico City. What is the mountain's Aztec name?
    Popocatepetl?
    Vesuvius?
    Dolores del Rio?
    Mountana Smokey?

3. What was the name of the Spanish adventurer who defeated the Aztecs in 1521 and captured Mexico for Spain?
    Hernando Cortes?
    Fernando Lopez?
    Aino Corrida?
    Jose Portillo?

WHERE NEXT?

United States, Belize, Guatemala or Cuba.

Monaco

1. For seven hundred years the principality of Monaco has been ruled by one family. What is the family's name?
    Rainier?
    Carlo?
    Larvotto?
    Grimaldi?

2. Prince Rainier III of Monaco succeeded his grandfather in 1949. Who will succeed Prince Rainier?
    Prince Albert?
    Princess Caroline?
    Princess Stephanie?
    Princess Grace?

3. Prince Rainier and Grace Kelly were married on 19th April. In which year?
    1952?
    1954?
    1956?
    1958?

WHERE NEXT?

France or Italy.

Mongolia

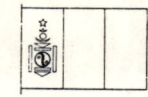

1. **When did the Mongol conqueror Genghis Khan live?**
   865 to 942?
   1162 to 1227?
   1401 to 1480?
   1553 to 1627?

2. **The area of Mongolia exceeds 600,000 square miles. What is the country's population?**
   Around 1,500,000?
   Around 15,000,000?
   Around 150,000,000?
   Around 210,000,000?

3. **Mongolia is a buffer state between China and the Soviet Union. On which country is it dependent for massive aid and trade?**
   China?
   Soviet Union?
   Neither: Mongolia manages to maintain complete independence?

WHERE NEXT?

China or Soviet Union.

Morocco

1. **Who said, 'Like Webster's Dictionary, we're Morocco bound'?**
    King Faisal?
    Rommel?
    Bob Hope?
    Thomas Webster?

2. **Who is Morocco's Head of State?**
    President Ahmed Osman?
    King Hassan II?
    Sheikh Mohamed Benhima?
    Dr Ahmed Laraki?

3. **Humphrey Bogart and Ingrid Bergman starred in a 1943 film set in a Moroccan city. Which one?**
    Tangier?
    Marrakesh?
    Rabat?
    Casablanca?

WHERE NEXT?

Western Sahara, Portugal, Spain, Algeria or Mauritania.

Mozambique

1. **In Mozambique, how do they spell Mozambique?**
    Moçambique?
    Mossambique?
    Mutzimbeak?
    Manana?

2. **Maputo is the country's capital. What was it once called?**
    Lourenço Marques?
    Washington?
    Frelimo?
    Cabora Bassa?

3. **The man who discovered the sea route to India in 1498 also discovered Mozambique. What was his name?**
    Ferdinand Magellan?
    Vasco da Gama?
    Manuel Garcia?
    Lope de Vega?

WHERE NEXT?

Tanzania, Malawi, Zambia, Zimbabwe or South Africa.

Nauru

1. **In 1968 Nauru became an independent republic within the Commonwealth. Who is its Head of State?**
    Queen Elizabeth II?
    President Hammer de Roburt?
    Emperor Manuel del Figes?
    The Prime Minister of Australia?

2. **What is the population of Nauru?**
    Over 7,000?
    Over 70,000?
    Over 700,000?
    Over 7,000,000?

3. **The island's economy depends entirely on the exploitation of one resource – and that will probably be exhausted by 1992. What is it?**
    Iron ore?
    Phosphates?
    Oil?
    Coral?

WHERE NEXT?

Gilbert Islands, Fiji, Papua New Guinea or Australia.

Nepal

1. **Nepalese troops have served Britain well. What are they called?**
    The Blues?
    The Royals?
    The Neps?
    The Gurkhas?

2. **In January 1972 King Birendra succeeded his father as Nepalese Head of State. What was his father called?**
    King Mahendra?
    King Kabool?
    King Bohindra?
    King Saize?

3. **Everest, the world's highest mountain, is in Nepal. How high is it?**
    19,028 ft?
    29,028 ft?
    39,028 ft?
    49,028 ft?

WHERE NEXT?

China or India.

Netherlands

1. **Amsterdam is the capital of the Netherlands, but in which Dutch city is the government based?**
    Amsterdam?
    The Hague?
    Rotterdam?
    Utrecht?

2. **There is one everyday product of which the Dutch are the world's largest exporters. What is it?**
    Tulips?
    Cheese?
    Cassette recorders?
    Eggs?

3. **Queen Juliana came to the Dutch throne on 4 September 1948. Why?**
    Her father the King was assassinated?
    Her father the King died?
    Her mother the Queen was killed in an air crash?
    Her mother the Queen abdicated?

WHERE NEXT?

Belgium or West Germany.

New Zealand

1. **Who was it who discovered New Zealand in 1642?**
     Enrico Zealand?
     Thomas Cook?
     William Budd?
     Abel Tasman?

2. **Of the islands that make up New Zealand the largest covers 58,093 square miles. What is it called?**
     South Island?
     North Island?
     Stewart Island?
     Chatham Island?

3. **Roughly what percentage of the New Zealand population are Maoris?**
     1%?
     7%?
     16%?
     29%?

WHERE NEXT?

Australia.

Nicaragua

1. **Nicaragua boasts the largest lake in Central America. It's 100 miles long and up to 42 miles wide. What is it called?**
    Lake Granada?
    Lake Bianca?
    Lake Worth?
    Lake Nicaragua?

2. **Two rival families have traditionally ruled Nicaragua. One is the Chamarro family. The other family has been in power for over 30 years (the head of the family is President) and controls the army and many of the country's commercial interests, including the air and shipping lines. What is the family's name?**
    Somoza?
    Taramosalata?
    Sheftalia?
    Horez?

3. **What is the capital of Nicaragua?**
    Managua?
    Leon?
    Bonanza?
    Chinandega?

WHERE NEXT?

Honduras or Costa Rica.

Niger

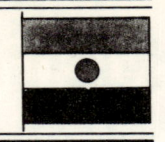

1. Niger covers some 460,000 square miles. What characterises most of that territory?
    - Swamps?
    - The Zinder forests?
    - Mountains?
    - The Sahara desert?

2. They speak Arabic and Hausa in Niger, but what is the official language?
    - English?
    - French?
    - Bilma?
    - Niger?

3. What was the name of the President of Niger, who led the country from the time of independence until his overthrow in 1974?
    - Hamani?
    - Salami?
    - Biriyani?
    - Radani?

WHERE NEXT?

Algeria, Libya, Chad, Nigeria, Benin, Voltaic Republic or Mali.

Nigeria

1. Who was Nigeria's first Prime Minister?
    General Gowon?
    Colonel Ojukwu?
    Dr Hastings Banda?
    Sir Abubakar Tafewa Balewa?

2. What was the name of the part of Nigeria that attempted secession in 1967, but was finally defeated in 1970?
    Lagos?
    Ibadan?
    Kano?
    Biafra?

3. Within Nigeria there are many tribes, three of the main ones being the Yoruba, Hausa and Fulani. What is the name of another of the four principal tribes?
    Ibo?
    Abo?
    Ubu?
    Roi?

WHERE NEXT?

Niger, Chad, Cameroon or Benin.

North Korea

1. **What is the line that divides North and South Korea?**
    The 16th parallel?
    The 27th parallel?
    The 38th parallel?
    The 49th parallel?

2. **The Korean War began as a result of the North invading the South on 25 June in a certain year. Which year?**
    1949?
    1950?
    1951?
    1952?

3. **Who is the President of the Democratic People's Republic of Korea?**
    Kim Il Sung?
    Leonid Brezhnev?
    Lee Duc Tho?
    Kim Kum Koo?

WHERE NEXT?

South Korea, Soviet Union, China or Japan.

Norway

1. **What is the Norwegian parliament called?**
    The Storting?
    The Bundestag?
    The Wundertang?
    The Voting?

2. **From 1397 to 1814 Norway was united with which other European country?**
    Sweden?
    Denmark?
    Finland?
    Russia?

3. **The Norwegian author of *The Master Builder, The Wild Duck, Peer Gynt* and other plays, was born in 1828 and died in 1906. What was his name?**
    August Strindberg?
    Henrik Ibsen?
    Henrik Wergeland?
    Otto von Bismarck?

WHERE NEXT?

Sweden, Finland, Denmark or Iceland.

Oman

1. The Al bu Said dynasty has ruled in the Oman since 1747. The present Sultan, Qaboos bin Said, has been Sultan since 1970, when he succeeded his father. What happened to the father?
   Did he die in his sleep?
   Was he deposed by his son?
   Was he murdered?
   Did he commit suicide?

2. What is the capital of Oman?
   Dili?
   Riyadh?
   Doha?
   Muscat?

3. Britain has a defence treaty with Oman and an R.A.F. staging post on an island just off Oman's east coast. What is the island called?
   Masira?
   Tokay?
   Nizwa?
   Rafia?

   WHERE NEXT?

   Iran, South Yemen, Saudi Arabia or United Arab Emirates.

Pakistan

1. **Who was the 'founder' of Pakistan who died in 1948?**
    Gandhi?
    Jinnah?
    Bhutto?
    Nehru?

2. **Who became President of Pakistan after an army *coup* in 1958 and resigned in 1969?**
    Ayub Khan?
    Yahya Khan?
    Aga Khan?
    Ali Khan?

3. **In which city in Pakistan will you find the Shalimar Gardens and the Badshahi Mosque, the largest mosque in the world?**
    Islamabad?
    Karachi?
    Lahore?
    Hyderabad?

WHERE NEXT?

India, Iran, Afghanistan, Soviet Union or China.

Panama

1. **When wearing a 'panama' what are you dressed in?**
   A grass skirt?
   A Central American belt?
   A bow tie?
   A hat?

2. **When was the Panama Canal built?**
   1852–1860?
   1876–1887?
   1904–1914?
   1918–1923?

3. **Since 1968 the Commander of the National Guard has been Panama's ruler. What's his name?**
   General Omar Torrijos?
   General Omar Bradley?
   Colonel Arnulfo Arias?
   Colonel Roberto Migueze?

WHERE NEXT?

Costa Rica or Colombia.

Papua New Guinea

1. Papua New Guinea consists of many islands, the largest of which is the island of New Guinea itself. It is the third largest island in the world, after Australia and Greenland. What is the fourth largest island in the world?
    Borneo?
    Baffin Island?
    Sumatra?
    Britain?

2. Only the eastern half of the island of New Guinea is part of the country of Papua New Guinea. To whom does the western half belong?
    Australia?
    Indonesia?
    Philippines?
    Malaysia?

3. What is the principal language spoken in Papua New Guinea?
    English?
    Papuan?
    Indonesian?
    Spanish?

WHERE NEXT?

Australia, Indonesia or Philippines.

Paraguay

1. **Paraguay has had the same dictator since 1954. What's his name?**
   Colonel Bogey?
   General Stroessner?
   Field-Marshal Pepe?
   President Suares?

2. **What is the capital of Paraguay?**
   Asuncion?
   Concepcion?
   San Pedro?
   Caracas?

3. **Spanish is one of Paraguay's two languages. Most Paraguayans are bilingual. What is the second language that most of them speak and that many prefer to Spanish?**
   English?
   French?
   Guarani?
   Pindi?

WHERE NEXT?

Bolivia, Brazil or Argentina.

Peru

1. In Lima Cathedral you can see the mummy of the Spanish adventurer who conquered Peru for Spain. He was murdered by his own men in 1541. What was his name?
    Pizarro?
    Dromego?
    Castillo?
    Gondolfo?

2. The ruins and remains of which great civilisation can be seen in Peru?
    The Mayan civilisation?
    The Inca civilisation?
    The Nomadic civilisation?
    The Ancient Greek civilisation?

3. There is a well-known Peruvian who is best known in England for his goonish, not to say potty, sense of humour. He was born in 1922. What's he called?
    Jacques Tati?
    Spike Milligan?
    Billy Connolly?
    Michael Bentine?

WHERE NEXT?

Ecuador, Colombia, Brazil, Bolivia or Chile.

Philippines

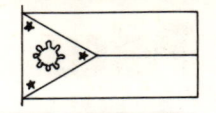

1. **In 1898 the United States bought the Philippines from Spain. How much did they pay?**
    20 dollars?
    200,000 dollars?
    20,000,000 dollars?
    100,000,000 dollars?

2. **The principal language of the Filipinos is very like Malay, but it has a different name. What is it?**
    Pilipino?
    Pidgin Malay?
    Huppupup?
    Luzon?

3. **What is the capital of the Philippines?**
    Quezon City?
    Marcos?
    Robesville?
    Manila?

WHERE NEXT?

Taiwan, Hong Kong, China, Vietnam, Malaysia or Indonesia.

Poland

1. **Ignace Jan Paderewski (1860–1941) was the first Prime Minister of a reconstituted Poland after the Great War. Apart from being Prime Minister, for what was Paderewski famous?**
    His unique stamp collection?
    His ability to speak 19 different languages?
    His success as a Grand Prix racing driver?
    His piano playing?

2. **A Polish composer was born in 1810 and died of consumption in 1849. He was born in Zova Vola, with a Polish mother and a French father. What was his name?**
    Lizst?
    Chopin?
    Weill?
    Debussy?

3. **The founder of modern astronomy was born in Torun in Poland in 1473 and died at Cracow in Poland in 1543. He wrote *On the Revolution of the Celestial Orbs*. What was his name?**
    Galileo?
    Newton?
    Copernicus?
    Flamsteed?

WHERE NEXT?

Soviet Union, Czechoslovakia or East Germany.

139

Portugal

1. From the eleventh century until 1910, the government of Portugal was a monarchy, and for many centuries included the Vice-Royalty of another country almost a hundred times its size! What was that other country?
    China?
    Spain?
    Afghanistan?
    Brazil?

2. From 1932 until he resigned in 1968 who ruled Portugal?
    General Franco?
    General Spinola?
    Dr Salazar?
    Admiral Tomas?

3. The second largest city in Portugal is famous for its vast wine cellars and for the particular wine that bears its name. What is the city called?
    Chianti?
    Spumante?
    Pernod?
    Oporto?

WHERE NEXT?

Spain or Morocco.

Qatar

1. **What is the capital of Qatar?**
    Qatar City?
    Doha?
    Sunni?
    Dukhan?

2. **Qatar is a member of OPEC. What do these initials stand for?**
    Oil Production Energy Council?
    Oil Producers Exploitation Consortium?
    Oil Producing Exporters Congress?
    Organisation of Petroleum Exporting Countries?

3. **What is the principal language of Qatar?**
    Qatari?
    Saudi?
    Persian?
    Arabic?

WHERE NEXT?

Bahrain, Saudi Arabia, United Arab Emirates or Iran.

Rumania

1. **Who is the President of Rumania?**
    President Gierek?
    President Hoxha?
    President Stoica?
    President Ceausescu?

2. **A Latin poet, who is best remembered for his *Metamorphoses*, was exiled to the Rumanian town of Constanta. What was his name?**
    Livy?
    Ovid?
    Homer?
    Virgil?

3. **Rumania's east coast is washed by which sea?**
    The Red Sea?
    The Black Sea?
    The Mediterranean Sea?
    The Caspian Sea?

WHERE NEXT?

Soviet Union, Hungary, Yugoslavia or Bulgaria.

Rwanda

1. Rwanda is the northern half of the former Belgian trusteeship of Ruanda-Urundi, which was divided on independence in 1962. What happened to Urundi? Is it now:
    Uganda?
    Urundi?
    Burundi?
    Tanzania?

2. From which other country did Belgium take Ruanda-Urundi in 1917?
    Britain?
    Germany?
    France?
    Spain?

3. What kind of Head of State had there been in the country until the people voted against his retention in 1961. Was there:
    A monarch?
    A President?
    A tribal chief?
    A witch-doctor?

WHERE NEXT?

Uganda, Tanzania, Burundi or Zaïre.

San Marino

1. The Most Serene Republic of San Marino claims to be the oldest state in Europe. When was it founded?
    200 B.C.?
    A.D. 301?
    A.D. 867?
    A.D. 1104?

2. San Marino has three castles, a church, a theatre and a museum. How many square miles does the country cover?
    12?
    24?
    48?
    160?

3. San Marino is in the hills near a popular seaside resort on the Adriatic coast. What is the resort called?
    Pisa?
    Bologna?
    Rimini?
    Naples?

WHERE NEXT?

Italy.

São Tomé and Príncipe

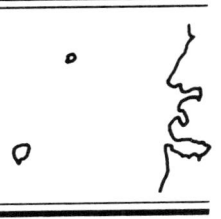

1. Where would you find the islands of São Tomé and Príncipe?
    The Gulf of Guinea?
    The Bay of Biscay?
    The Irish Sea?
    The Magellan Straits?

2. The islands were discovered in the year that Edward IV defeated and killed Warwick at Barnet and defeated Queen Margaret and Prince Edward of Wales at Tewkesbury. It was the same year that Henry VI was murdered in the Tower. What year was it?
    1371?
    1471?
    1571?
    1671?

3. The islands were a base for which notorious trade in the seventeenth and eighteenth centuries?
    The opium trade?
    The ivory trade?
    The cocaine trade?
    The slave trade?

WHERE NEXT?

Nigeria, Cameroon, Equatorial Guinea or Gabon.

Saudi Arabia

1. **What happened to King Faisal of Saudi Arabia in 1975? Was he:**
   Elected chairman of the Pan-Arab League?
   Crowned in an elaborate ceremony in Riyadh?
   Married for the tenth time?
   Assassinated?

2. **Of all the Middle Eastern States which one is the largest oil producer?**
   Saudi Arabia?
   Jordan?
   United Arab Emirates?
   Iran?

3. **The birthplace of Mohammed is in Saudi Arabia. It is the holiest city of Islam. What is it called?**
   Baghdad?
   Jerusalem?
   Mohamet?
   Mecca?

WHERE NEXT?

United Arab Emirates, Oman, Southern Yemen, Yemen, Jordan, Iraq or Kuwait.

Senegal

1. In the year that Queen Victoria married Prince Albert, the French first occupied Senegal. What was the year?
    1832?
    1837?
    1840?
    1850?

2. In the year that Princess Margaret married Antony Armstrong-Jones, Senegal became an independent member of the United Nations. What was the year?
    1955?
    1960?
    1963?
    1969?

3. Leopold Senghor has been President of Senegal since 1960. For what other acccomplishment is he famous in Africa?
    As a boxer?
    As a pilot?
    As an authority on voodoo?
    As a poet?

WHERE NEXT?

Gambia, Guinea, Mali or Mauritania.

147

Seychelles

1. **Apart from English and French, what language do they speak in the Seychelles?**
   Creole?
   Seychellese?
   Hamoo?
   Greek?

2. **The capital is Victoria, on the largest and most important of the islands in the Seychelles. What is the island called?**
   Mahé?
   Praslin?
   La Digue?
   Silhouette?

3. **What trees are particularly associated with the islands?**
   Dutch elms?
   Firs?
   Palms?
   Apple trees?

WHERE NEXT?

Tanzania, Mozambique, Madagascar or Mauritius.

Sierra Leone

1. **The British founded this former colony in 1787. Why?**
   To be able to exploit the copper mines?
   To use it as a base for missionary work on the west coast of Africa?
   To provide a colony for destitute slaves?
   To use it as a base for pearl-fishing?

2. **Conditions were once so unhealthy and hygiene so poor in this part of Africa, that explorers and settlers had a special phrase that they used to describe the area around Sierra Leone. What was it?**
   'The white man's grave'?
   'The black hole'?
   'Africa's hell'?
   'The black spot'?

3. **What is the capital of Sierra Leone?**
   Malabo?
   Nairobi?
   Freetown?
   Mogadishoo?

WHERE NEXT?

Guinea or Liberia.

Singapore

1. **Who founded Singapore in 1819?**
    Sir Stanley Matthews?
    Sir Henry Stanley?
    Sir Ralph O'Henry?
    Sir Stamford Raffles?

2. **Who is Singapore's Head of State?**
    Prime Minister Lee Kuan Yew?
    President Benjamin Sheares?
    Queen Elizabeth II?
    Prince Goh Keng Swee Tung Su Rajaratnam Sung Song Fah?

3. **Singapore is the name of the country, of the country's capital and of the country's principal island. Apart from the island of Singapore, how many other islands are there in Singapore?**
    5?
    15?
    24?
    54?

WHERE NEXT?

Malaysia or Indonesia.

Solomon Islands

1. **Excluding the northern islands of Bougainville and Buka, the rest of the Solomon Islands have been under the protection of which country since 1893?**
    Japan?
    United Kingdom?
    Australia?
    The United States?

2. **The capital is on the island of Guadalcanal. During the Second World War it was the headquarters of the Western Pacific High Commission. What is it called?**
    Honiara?
    Bellona?
    Vanikolo?
    Tikopia?

3. **What sort of terrain do you find over most of the Solomon Islands?**
    Mountainous and covered with rain forests?
    Desert?
    Flat and tropical?
    Covered with rice fields?

WHERE NEXT?

Papua New Guinea or Australia.

Somalia

1. **The Somali Democratic Republic's position on the African continent has led to a particular phrase being used to describe the country's precise location. What is the phrase?**
   The Elbow of Africa?
   The Shoe of Africa?
   The Rump of Africa?
   The Horn of Africa?

2. **What was the natural disaster that afflicted Somalia between 1969 and 1975?**
   Earthquakes?
   The plague?
   Drought?
   Swine fever?

3. **Since independence the Republic has received aid from many quarters (the United Nations, the European Economic Community, Italy, Libya and others) but the major aid, including arms and military 'advisers', has come from which country?**
   China?
   Soviet Union?
   United States?
   Egypt?

WHERE NEXT?

Ethiopia or Kenya.

South Africa

1. **What percentage of the population of South Africa are white Europeans?**
   2%?
   10%?
   17%?
   25%?

2. **He was born in 1870 and died in 1950. During the Boer war he fought on the Boer side and was Prime Minister of the Union of South Africa from 1919 to 1924 and from 1939 to 1948. What was his name?**
   Jan Smuts?
   Hendrik Voerwoerd?
   Stephanus Kruger?
   John Vorster?

3. **In 1976 South Africa granted token independence to South West Africa and South West Africa then changed its name. What is it now called?**
   Bantustan?
   Lesotho?
   Transvaal?
   Namibia?

WHERE NEXT?

Lesotho, Botswana, Zimbabwe, Mozambique or Swaziland.

South Korea

1. **Who ruled Korea between 1904 and 1945?**
   United States?
   Japan?
   China?
   France?

2. **Who was President of the Republic of Korea from 1948 until 1960 when he was eighty-five?**
   Syngman Rhee?
   Park Chung Hee?
   Kim Il Song?
   Chu Chin Chow?

3. **What is the currency used in South Korea?**
   The won?
   The Korean dollar?
   The seoul?
   The Korean franc?

   WHERE NEXT?

   North Korea or Japan.

South Yemen

1. The People's Democratic Republic of Yemen was formerly the South Arabian Federation. Part of the Federation was a former British Crown Colony that was one of the world's largest oil ports. What was its name?
    Dubai?
    Mukalla?
    Aden?
    Gulf?

2. Britain withdrew from the area in the year that Jeremy Thorpe became leader of the Liberal party, that Britain had its first colour television programmes and that Che Guevara was killed. What year was that?
    1958?
    1962?
    1967?
    1971?

3. What is the political complexion of South Yemen today? Is it a:
    Communist republic?
    Democratic republic?
    Fascist republic?
    Chinese satellite disguised as a Democratic republic?

WHERE NEXT?

Oman, Saudi Arabia or Yemen.

Soviet Union

1. **What do the initials U.S.S.R. stand for?**
   Union of Soviet States of Russia?
   United Socialist Soviets of Russia?
   United States of Soviet Russia?
   Union of Soviet Socialist Republics?

2. **Who has been President of the Soviet Union since 1965?**
   Nikolay Podgorny?
   Leonid Brezhnev?
   Alexei Kosygin?
   Andrei Gromyko?

3. **What is the name of the great nineteenth-century Russian writer whose masterpieces include *War and Peace* and *Anna Karenina*?**
   Leo Tolstoy?
   Feodor Dostoyevsky?
   Maxim Gorky?
   Nikolai Gogol?

WHERE NEXT?

Finland, Poland, Czechoslovakia, Hungary, Rumania,

Spain

1. Cervantes, the great Spanish novelist and dramatist, was born at Alcala de Henares in 1547. His masterpiece *Don Quixote* describes the adventures of 'the knight of the woeful countenance'. On his travels, who was Don Quixote's companion? Was it:
    Rosinante?
    Sancho Panza?
    Ricardo Kiley?
    Adolfo Suarez?

2. Goya (1746–1828) was one of Spain's greatest painters. What happened to his portrait of the Duke of Wellington in 1961? Was it:
    Given to Britain by Spain?
    Mutilated in the Tate Gallery by a Basque Nationalist?
    Revealed as the work of another artist?
    Stolen from the National Gallery in London?

3. What is the Spanish parliament called?
    El Parliamento?
    The Carrero Blanco?
    The Cortes?
    The Communardo?

WHERE NEXT?

France, Andorra, Portugal, Morocco or Gibraltar.

Sri Lanka

1. **When did Ceylon become Sri Lanka?**
    1958?
    1965?
    1972?
    1975?

2. **What are Sri Lanka's three major exports?**
    Cotton, silk and rice?
    Cinnamon, graphite and sapphires?
    Tea, rubber and coconuts?
    Bananas, coffee and rice paper?

3. **Sri Lanka had one of the world's very first female Prime Ministers. She first came to office in 1960. What was her name?**
    Mrs Nehru?
    Mrs Gandhi?
    Mrs Bandaranaike?
    Mrs Senanayake?

WHERE NEXT?

India.

Sudan

1. **The word 'Sudan' is Arabic. What does it mean?**
    Sun-drenched?
    Desert?
    Northern star?
    Black?

2. **What was the name of the one-time Governor of the Sudan who was killed in 1885 by the Mahdist rebels in Khartoum?**
    General Haig?
    General Alexander?
    General Gordon?
    General Booth?

3. **The Mahdists destroyed Khartoum in 1885, but it was later recaptured by Anglo-Egyptian forces under Lord Kitchener. Kitchener drafted a new layout for the city, which is the capital of the Sudan. What unusual shape did he choose for the layout?**
    A star?
    A camel's hump?
    A crescent?
    The Union Jack?

WHERE NEXT?

Ethiopia, Kenya, Uganda, Zaïre, Central African Empire, Chad, Libya or Egypt.

Surinam

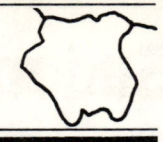

1. **Until independence Surinam was Dutch Guiana. How did the Dutch acquire the country in 1667?**
   Conquer it?
   Buy it from the French?
   Capture it from the Aztecs?
   Receive it as a gift from Britain in return for giving Britain what is now New York?

2. **What is the capital of Surinam?**
   Paramaribo?
   Manirus?
   Cayenne?
   La Paz?

3. **Surinam covers some 62,500 square miles. It claims a further 6,000 square miles of another country. Which one?**
   Guyana?
   Guiana?
   Brazil?
   Bolivia?

WHERE NEXT?

French Guiana, Guyana or Brazil.

Swaziland

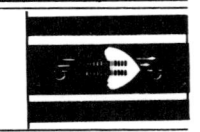

1. **Who is Swaziland's Head of State?**
    Queen Elizabeth II?
    King Sobhuza II?
    President Nganwe?
    Chief David?

2. **In Swaziland both Swazi and South African currency are legal tender, but the local unit of currency is the lilangeni. What is the plural of lilangeni?**
    Lilangenis?
    Muchlilangeni?
    Lilangeniooooo?
    Emalangeri?

3. **What is the capital of Swaziland?**
    Mbabane?
    Manzini?
    Pretoria?
    Diamini?

    WHERE NEXT?

    South Africa or Mozambique.

Sweden

1. The world's longest canal is in Sweden. It runs 115 miles, is 10 ft deep, 47 ft wide and was built in 1832. What's it called?
    The Swedish Canal?
    The Gota Canal?
    The Welland Canal?
    The Kiel Canal?

2. Alfred Nobel, founder of the Nobel prizes, was a Swede who lived from 1833 to 1896. Apart from his philanthropy, how is Nobel remembered?
    As the inventor of photography?
    As the discoverer of dynamite?
    As the hotelier who founded the Savoy and the Ritz?
    As the author of *Das Kapital*?

3. Sweden had the same Prime Minister from 1946 to 1969. It was the longest period in office enjoyed by any European Prime Minister. What was the man's name?
    Olaf Palme?
    Tage Erlander?
    Odvar Nordli?
    Dag Hammarskjold?

WHERE NEXT?

Norway, Finland or Denmark.

Switzerland

1. Switzerland boasts four national languages. Swiss German, French and Italian are three of them. What is the fourth?
   Austrian?
   Spanish?
   Frisch?
   Romansch?

2. Since when have women in Switzerland been allowed to vote in the Federal elections?
   1897?
   1948?
   1971?
   They haven't: in all but two cantons, Swiss women still do not have the vote?

3. Geneva University was founded in 1559 by a famous French Protestant reformer and theologian. Who was he?
   Blaise Pascal?
   Martin Luther?
   Jean Jacques Rousseau?
   John Calvin?

WHERE NEXT?

Italy, France, West Germany or Austria.

Syria

1. Syria is bounded by Turkey, Iraq, Jordan, Israel, Lebanon and a sea. Which sea?
    - The Red Sea?
    - The Dead Sea?
    - The Arabian Sea?
    - The Mediterranean Sea?

2. During the Six-Day War with Israel in 1967, which principal part of its territory was lost to Syria?
    - Damascus?
    - Palmyra?
    - Aleppo?
    - The Golan Heights?

3. In Damascus, reputed to be the oldest continuously inhabited city in the world, you will find the tomb of a sultan of Egypt and Syria who in 1187 defeated the Christians near Tiberias and took Jerusalem, an action which led to the Third Crusade. What was his name?
    - Tamburlaine?
    - Alexander the Great?
    - Saladin?
    - Sindbad?

WHERE NEXT?

Turkey, Iraq, Jordan, Israel or Lebanon.

Taiwan

1. **A number of islands make up modern Taiwan. The name of the largest of the islands, discovered by the Portuguese in 1590, is the name traditionally given to the group. What is it?**
    Singapore?
    Taipei?
    Matsu?
    Formosa?

2. **In 1949 Taiwan became the last refuge of the Chinese Nationalist government who fled there from the Chinese mainland. Their leader died in April 1975, aged 89. What was his name?**
    Chou en Lai?
    Mao Tse Tung?
    Lin Piau?
    Chiang Kai-shek?

3. **What happened to Taiwan at the United Nations in 1972? Was Taiwan:**
    Given a seat for the first time?
    Expelled so that mainland China could have a seat on the Security Council?
    Forced to agree to attend the U.N. alternate years, so that Communist China would be represented one year and Nationalist China represented the next?
    Or, was the then Prime Minister of Taiwan, Yen Chia Ken, elected Secretary General of the U.N.?

WHERE NEXT?

China, Japan, Hong Kong or Vietnam.

Tanzania

1. **Tanzania combines two countries. Tanganyika is one of them. What is the other?**
    Southern Rhodesia?
    Angola?
    Somalia?
    Zanzibar?

2. **An extinct volcano in Tanzania gives Africa her highest peak. What is the volcano called?**
    Mount Lumumba?
    Mount Orion?
    Mount Kilimanjaro?
    Mount Etna?

3. **President Nyerere was first elected in 1962. He was re-elected in 1965, 1970 and 1975. What is his first name?**
    Kenneth?
    Ngabe?
    Mrisho?
    Julius?

WHERE NEXT?

Mozambique, Malawi, Zambia, Zaïre, Burundi, Rwanda or Kenya.

Thailand

1. When was the coronation of the first King of Siam? Was it in:
    1350?
    1650?
    1850?
    1950?

2. The first film of *Anna and the King of Siam* was made in 1946 and starred Rex Harrison and Linda Darnell. Ten years later there was a musical version called *The King and I*. Yul Brynner played the King. Who played Anna?
    Ingrid Bergman?
    Ginger Rogers?
    Julie Andrews?
    Deborah Kerr?

3. Krung Thep is what the modern Thai calls his capital city. How is Krung Thep also known?
    Rangoon?
    Pyongyang?
    Kuching?
    Bangkok?

WHERE NEXT?

Laos, Kampuchea, Malaysia or Burma.

Togo

1. An important Convention, agreed between 46 African, Pacific and Caribbean countries and the European Economic Community, was signed in Togo's capital in 1975. What is the Convention called?
   - The Togo Convention?
   - The Euro-Afric Convention?
   - The Lomé Convention?
   - The Gulf of Guinea Convention?

2. Togo was formerly part of German Togoland. From the time of the First World War until Togo's independence in 1960, who administered the country?
   - Germany?
   - France?
   - Britain?
   - Spain?

3. What is the governmental system now operating in Togo?
   - Parliamentary democracy?
   - Military dictatorship?
   - Federal commonwealth?
   - Constitutional monarchy?

WHERE NEXT?

Benin, Ghana or Voltaic Republic.

Tonga

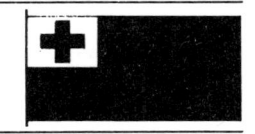

1. **How are the Tonga islands also known?**
    The Banana Islands?
    The South Pacific Islands?
    The Friendly Islands?
    The Sunshine Islands?

2. **What was the name of the famous Queen of Tonga who was succeeded by the present King in 1965?**
    Elizabeth?
    Rotunda?
    Heloise?
    Salote?

3. **Abel Tasman discovered Tongatapu, the main island, in the year of the Battle of Atherton Moor when Charles I issued the first English medals for gallantry. What year was it?**
    1470?
    1643?
    1750?
    1796?

WHERE NEXT?

Australia, New Zealand or Papua New Guinea.

Trinidad and Tobago

1. **What is the capital of Trinidad and Tobago?**
    Port-au-Prince?
    Port of France?
    Port of Spain?
    Oporto?

2. **Trinidad is an island off the coast of which South American country?**
    Venezuela?
    Guyana?
    Colombia?
    Surinam?

3. **In 1956 he first became Trinidad's Chief Minister. Now he is Prime Minister. What's his name?**
    Eric Gairy?
    John Milton?
    Eric Williams?
    John Junor?

WHERE NEXT?

Venezuela, Guyana, Dominican Republic or Haiti.

Tunisia

1. When Tunisia became independent in 1956, he was Prime Minister. He became President in 1957. What's his name?
    Sadat?
    Nouira?
    Boumédienne?
    Bourguiba?

2. Just nine miles out of Tunis you can see the ruins of which great ancient city?
    Persepolis?
    Tyre?
    Carthage?
    Dunstable?

3. What is the unit of currency in Tunisia?
    The alexander?
    The tunis?
    The dinar?
    The Tunisian dollar?

WHERE NEXT?

Italy, Malta, Algeria or Libya.

Turkey

1. **In the past, Istanbul has been known by another name. What is it?**
    Ankara?
    Izmir?
    Constantinople?
    Byzantium?

2. **Who was the leader who declared the Turkish Republic in 1923 and became its first President?**
    Fabri Koroturk?
    Kemal Ataturk?
    Nihat Erim?
    Ismet Inonu?

3. **One of the world's most spectacular and beautiful buildings is in Istanbul. It was built by Justinian in the sixth century as a church and was later converted into a mosque. What's it called?**
    Topkapi Palace?
    St Sophia?
    Temple of Augustus?
    Citadel?

WHERE NEXT?

Soviet Union, Iran, Iraq, Syria, Cyprus, Greece, Bulgaria or Rumania.

Uganda

1. **What is the name of the British writer and editor of *Punch* who has published two best-selling volumes of parodies of the thoughts of President Idi Amin?**
    Malcolm Muggeridge?
    Patrick Campbell?
    Alan Coren?
    Frank Muir?

2. **Part of the third largest lake in the world is in Uganda. What's it called?**
    Lake Superior?
    Lake Nyasa?
    Lake Niger?
    Lake Victoria?

3. **What is the capital of Uganda?**
    Entebbe?
    Obote?
    Masaka?
    Kampala?

   WHERE NEXT?

   Sudan, Kenya, Rwanda or Zaïre.

United Arab Emirates

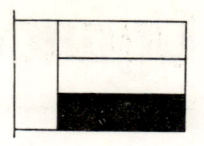

1. The United Arab Emirates is a union of seven Emirates. Dubai, Sharjah, Ajman, Ras al Khaimah, Umm al Qawain and Fujairah are six of them. What is the seventh? It is also the most powerful, the most populous and the richest in oil.
    Bahrain?
    Qatar?
    Oman?
    Abu Dhabi?

2. Before the formation of the union in 1971, how were the sheikdoms known?
    Arab Free States?
    Federation of Pan-Arab States?
    Desert States?
    Trucial States?

3. What is the principal religion found in the United Arab Emirates?
    Sunni Muslim?
    Mooniism?
    Buddhism?
    Bahaism?

WHERE NEXT?

Iran, Oman, Saudi Arabia or Qatar.

United Kingdom

1. **There are some 30,000 square miles to Scotland, some 8,000 square miles to Wales and some 5,000 square miles to Northern Ireland. Roughly how many square miles are there in England?**
    35,000?
    50,000?
    70,000?
    96,000?

2. **In whose reign was the British Constitution first written down?**
    In the reign of King John?
    In the reign of Richard II?
    In the reign of Elizabeth I?
    Never written down, because the British constitution is unwritten and based largely on convention and judicial and parliamentary decisions?

3. **Britain's longest river runs for 220 miles. What is it called?**
    The Thames?
    The Severn?
    The Trent?
    The Great Ouse?

WHERE NEXT?

Ireland, Netherlands, Belgium or France.

United States of America

1. **On the flag of the United States there are 50 stars (one for each state), but how many stripes? There is one for each of the original states of the union.**
   7?
   13?
   21?
   30?

2. **Abraham Lincoln was the first American President to be assassinated, John Kennedy the last. Between Lincoln and Kennedy, two other Presidents were assassinated. Who were they?**
   Garfield and McKinley?
   Jackson and Van Buren?
   Taylor and Grant?
   Hayes and Arthur?

3. **The second President of the United States was also the most long-lived. He died on 4 July 1826 at the age of 90. What was his name?**
   John Adams?
   Thomas Jefferson?
   James Madison?
   James Monroe?

WHERE NEXT?

Canada, Mexico or Cuba.

Uruguay

1. **What is the capital of Uruguay?**
   Montevideo?
   Caracas?
   Santiago?
   La Paz?

2. **In South American terms, what is special about Uruguay's size? Is it:**
   The smallest country on the continent?
   The largest country on the continent?
   The only country on the continent whose territory is entirely mountainous?
   The only country on the continent where more than half the area is covered with rivers and lakes?

3. **Uruguay shares an important river with Argentina. It was discovered by Diaz de Solis in 1516 and explored by Magellan in 1520. In December 1939 naval action took place off its mouth, after which the German pocket battleship the *Graf Spee* was scuttled because it was unable to leave the river. What's the river called?**
   The River Spee?
   The Amazon?
   The River Plate?
   The Rio de la Plata?

WHERE NEXT?

Brazil or Argentina.

Vatican City

1. **The Vatican City is an independent sovereign state with its own coinage, its own postage stamps and its own subjects. What is the population of the Vatican City?**
    About 100?
    About 1,000?
    About 10,000?
    About 100,000?

2. **What is the Pope's summer residence called?**
    Vatican-sur-Mer?
    Sistine Chapel?
    Castel Gandolfo?
    Castel St Angelo?

3. **In July 1968 Pope Paul VI issued an encyclical called *Humanae Vitae*. What was it about?**
    The ending of the Tridentine Mass?
    Women priests?
    The Ecumenical Council?
    Birth control?

WHERE NEXT?

Italy.

Venezuela

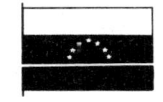

1. **Venezuela means 'Little Venice'. What is the origin of its name?**
   The original settlers came from Venice in Italy?
   The original settlers came from 'Little Venice' in North London?
   Many people lived in houses built on stilts over water?
   The fishermen on Lake Maracaibo use boats like gondolas?

2. **A man known as 'The Liberator' of South America was born in Caracas in 1783. Who was he?**
   Che Guevara?
   Simon Bolivar?
   Agustin de Iturbide?
   Juan Manuel de Rosas?

3. **What is the name of the major river which runs through Venezuela?**
   The Amazon?
   The River Plate?
   The Orinoco?
   The Araguaya?

WHERE NEXT?

Colombia, Guyana, Brazil or Trinidad and Tobago.

Vietnam

1. In what year was Vietnam reunited as a single country?
      1974?
      1975?
      1976?
      1977?

2. After the fall of South Vietnam, Saigon was renamed. What is its new name?
      Hanoi?
      Haiphong?
      Ho Chi Minh City?
      Mao Tse Tung City?

3. What is the line of latitude which separated the states of North and South Vietnam until the end of the Vietnamese War?
      The 49th parallel?
      The 19th parallel?
      The 17th parallel?
      The 31st parallel?

WHERE NEXT?

China, Laos or Kampuchea.

The Virgin Islands

1. **The Virgin Islands are divided into two groups. Which countries are they associated with?**
    Britain and the United States?
    Denmark and the Netherlands?
    Britain and France?
    France and Denmark?

2. **The Anegada Passage is strategically important because it is the main sea route to a vital communications link. Where does it lead to?**
    The Suez Canal?
    The Panama Canal?
    The Bering Straits?
    The Gulf of Mexico?

3. **How many islands are there in the group?**
    About 50?
    About 100?
    About 150?
    About 200?

    WHERE NEXT?

    Dominican Republic, Trinidad and Tobago or the Bahamas.

Voltaic Republic

1. **Until 1947 the Voltaic Republic was part of which other state?**
   Ghana?
   Togo?
   Mali?
   Ivory Coast?

2. **Which European country used to govern the area?**
   Italy?
   Spain?
   France?
   United Kingdom?

3. **What is the main ethnic group in the country?**
   The Masai?
   The Mossi?
   The Bantu?
   The Hamitics?

   WHERE NEXT?

   Mali, Niger, Benin, Togo, Ghana or Ivory Coast.

West Germany

1. **What is the correct name for West Germany?**
   The German Democratic Republic?
   The German Federal Republic?
   The German Free State?
   Germany?

2. **Bonn is the capital of Germany, but it only has a population of around 300,000. Which German city has the largest population?**
   West Berlin?
   Hamburg?
   Munich?
   Frankfurt?

3. **Who was the West German Chancellor from 1949 to 1963?**
   Walter Scheel?
   Helmut Schmidt?
   Willy Brandt?
   Konrad Adenauer?

WHERE NEXT?

Switzerland, France, Luxembourg, Belgium, Netherlands, Denmark, East Germany, Czechoslovakia or Austria.

West Indies Associated States

1. **Which of the islands was the first to be settled by the English?**
   St Kitts in 1623?
   Antigua in 1632?
   St Vincent in 1783?
   Dominica in 1789?

2. **Which explorer first discovered the islands?**
   Christopher Columbus?
   Sir Francis Drake?
   Henry the Navigator?
   Dr Livingstone?

3. **What is Grand Turk?**
   A tropical fish common in the area?
   A tropical bird common in the islands?
   One of the islands?
   One of the government officials?

WHERE NEXT?

Trinidad and Tobago, Venezuela or Barbados.

Western Sahara

1. What type of government does the Western Sahara have? Is it:
    Unsettled?
    A Spanish dominion?
    A republic?
    A monarchy?

2. Several countries have fought over the area because of its mineral wealth. It is particularly rich in one mineral. Which?
    Copper?
    Gold?
    Potash?
    Plutonium?

3. What is the name of the local liberation movement?
    W.S.L.M.?
    Polisario?
    Accion Democratica?
    Hamitic Liberation League?

WHERE NEXT?

Mauritania, Canary Islands or Morocco.

Western Samoa

1. **What are the names of the four main islands of Western Samoa?**
   Bobo, Dioulasso, Leo and Pama Ouahigouya?
   Nevis, St Lucia, St Vincent and Barbuda?
   Savai'i, Upolou, Manono and Apolima?
   Salto, Paysandu, Rivera and Melo?

2. **What famous man is buried there?**
   Gauguin?
   Robert Louis Stevenson?
   Noël Coward?
   Captain Cook?

3. **The Eastern Samoan Islands are under the sovereignty of which country?**
   New Zealand?
   New Guinea?
   United States?
   Australia?

WHERE NEXT?

Fiji, New Zealand, Australia or Papua New Guinea.

Yemen Arab Republic

1. **What is the official title of the Yemeni head of State?**
    First Party Secretary?
    Chairman of Command Council?
    Amir?
    Hereditary Grand Vizir?

2. **What is the main export product of the Yemen Arab Republic?**
    Coffee?
    Oil?
    Cotton?
    Copra?

3. **What was the ancient name of this area?**
    Sheba?
    Arabia Felix?
    Babel?
    Mesopotamia?

WHERE NEXT?

Ethiopia, Saudi Arabia, South Yemen or Somalia.

Yugoslavia

1. **Which is the largest ethnic group in Yugoslavia?**
    The Slovenes?
    The Serbs?
    The Montenegrins?
    The Croats?

2. **What is President Tito's first name?**
    Nikola?
    Ivo?
    Borislav?
    Josip?

3. **How many republics make up the State of Yugoslavia?**
    Two?
    Five?
    Six?
    Eleven?

WHERE NEXT?

Italy, Austria, Hungary, Rumania, Bulgaria, Greece or Albania.

Zaïre

1. **What is the capital of Zaïre?**
    Kinshasa?
    Zaïre City?
    Congola?
    Kananga?

2. **When did Zaïre become an independent republic?**
    June 1960?
    November 1958?
    August 1964?
    April 1950?

3. **Who was the first President of Zaïre?**
    King Baudouin?
    Tshombe?
    Kasavubu?
    Lumumba?

WHERE NEXT?

Angola, Gabon, Cameroon, Central African Empire, Sudan, Uganda, Rwanda, Burundi, Tanzania or Zambia.

Zambia

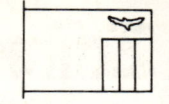

1. **Who is the President of Zambia?**
    John Vorster?
    Mobuto Seko?
    Mainza Chona?
    Kenneth Kaunda?

2. **Where in Zambia would you go to find the Victoria Falls?**
    Lusaka?
    Kitwe?
    Livingstone?
    Ndola?

3. **In November 1975 an important Chinese-built railway running through Zambia to Dar-es-Salaam was opened. What is it called?**
    The Trans-Zambia Railway?
    The Mao Railroad?
    The Tan-Zam Railway?
    The Lusaka Railroad?

WHERE NEXT?

Botswana, Angola, Zaïre, Tanzania, Malawi, Mozambique, or Zimbabwe.

Zimbabwe/Rhodesia

1. **Roughly what percentage of the population of Zimbabwe is European in origin?**
   1%?
   5%?
   10%?
   15%?

2. **You will find the Victoria Falls on the border between Zimbabwe and which other African country?**
   South Africa?
   Botswana?
   Zambia?
   Mozambique?

3. **Where in Zimbabwe would you go to find the world's largest colliery?**
   Bulawayo?
   Umtali?
   Salisbury?
   Wankie?

WHERE NEXT?

South Africa, Botswana, Zambia or Mozambique.

Answers

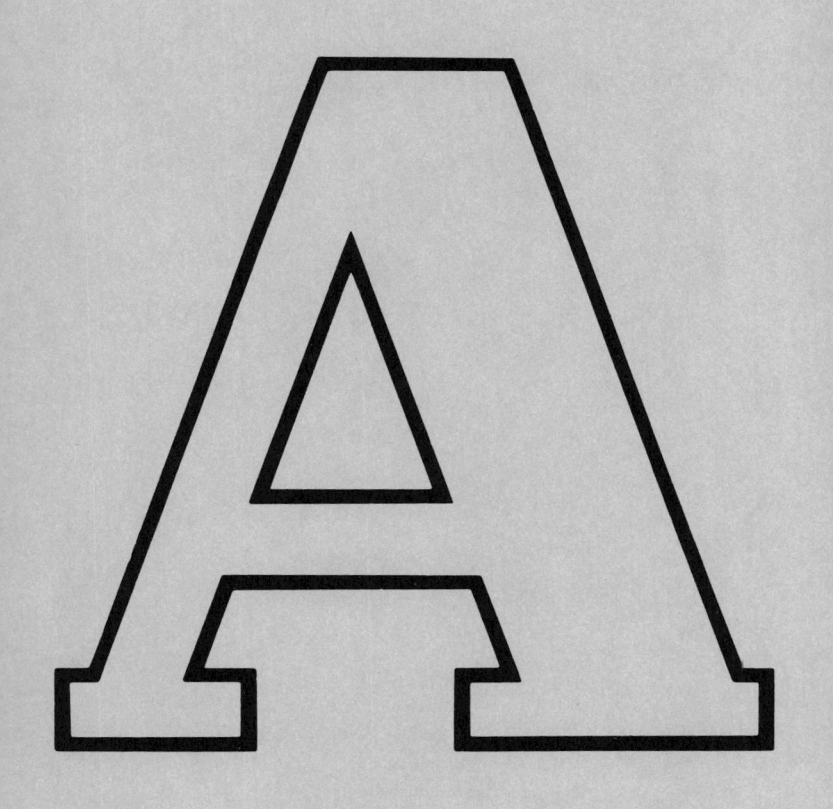

Answers

WHAT A WORLD!

1. Australia
2. Mandarin Chinese
3. The Pacific Ocean
4. Eric the Red
5. Ferdinand Magellan
6. 70%
7. Nine—the others are: Mercury, Venus, Mars, Jupiter, Saturn, Uranus, Neptune and Pluto
8. Shanghai, with over 10,000,000
9. Clouds
10. The Netherlands

AFGHANISTAN
Over nineteen million
Overthrown and assassinated
The afghani

ALBANIA
Tirana
The Ottoman Empire
King Zog

ALGERIA
1830
Ferhat Abbas
The Soviet Union

AMERICAN SAMOA
The Dutch in 1722
An American colony
Polynesian

ANDORRA
The President of France and the Spanish Bishop of Urgel
16,000
Max Frisch

ANGOLA
Luanda
Portugal
The Soviet Union and Cuba

ARGENTINA
1536
Meat
The Prince Edward

AUSTRALIA
Canberra
Harold Holt
1%

AUSTRIA
Salzburg
1918
The Danube

BAHAMAS
1492
About 20
Queen Elizabeth II

Answers

BAHRAIN
Pearl fishing
In 1990
Iran

BANGLADESH
Sheikh Mujib
Murdered by a group of army majors
Jute

BARBADOS
1639
The most easterly of the West Indies
Rum

BELGIUM
1830
Walloons
His father, King Leopold III, abdicated in his favour

BELIZE
British Honduras
Shipwrecked English sailors
Guatemala

BENIN
Dahomey
Black magic
Over 3,000,000

BERMUDA
It was discovered by Juan Bermudez in 1503
In return for destroyers needed for anti-submarine operations
Long shorts

BHUTAN
An hereditary monarch
Mahayana Buddhism
China

BOLIVIA
Sucre
1825
Che Guevara

BOTSWANA
Bechuanaland
Seretse Khama
Diamonds

BRAZIL
Brasilia
Coffee
The second largest river in the world

BRUNEI
The South China Sea
Sultan
The United Kingdom

BULGARIA
The Treaty of Berlin
Abolished by referendum
Cyrillic

BURMA
U Thant
The monsoons
Rangoon

BURUNDI
Belgium
Lake Tanganyika
Very tall

Answers

CAMEROON
France and Britain
13,350 ft
The Gulf of Guinea

CANADA
1964
19%
John Diefenbaker

THE CANARY ISLANDS
Spain
The islands were full of dogs
Las Palmas

CAPE VERDE ISLANDS
Off the West Coast of Africa
A Communist republic
The Soviet Union

CENTRAL AFRICAN EMPIRE
General Bokassa
Ubangi and Shari
Crown himself Emperor in the manner of Napoleon

CHAD
General Odingar
The Sahara Mountains
N'Djamene, formerly Fort Lamy

CHILE
Allende
Over 2,600 miles
The world's driest place where rain has never been recorded

CHINA
1911
900,000,000
Kubla Khan

COLOMBIA
Simon Bolivar
Le Corbusier
The peso

CONGO
Brazzaville
Angola
Middle Congo

COSTA RICA
A Presidential democracy
The country with the highest income *per capita* in Latin America
San José

CUBA
1898
Batista
1962

CYPRUS
Archbishop Makarios
78%
Copper

CZECHOSLOVAKIA
Bohemia and Moravia
1968
Dubček

DENMARK
Margrethe II
Danny Kaye
1972

Answers

DOMINICAN REPUBLIC
Haiti
Rafael Trujillo
Santo Domingo

EAST GERMANY
The German Democratic Republic
Over 3,600,000
1961

ECUADOR
Quito
Bananas
The sucre

EGYPT
30 B.C.
Farouk
Die of a heart attack

EL SALVADOR
San Salvador
Organisation of Central American States
Ecuador

EQUATORIAL GUINEA
A number of islands, the main one being Fernando Poo
Spain
Malabo, formerly Santa Isabel

ETHIOPIA
Solomon and the Queen of Sheba
'The Lion of Judah'
Eritrea

FIJI
322
Abel Tasman
Indian

FINLAND
Russia took it from Sweden
Sibelius
70%

FRANCE
7
About twice the size
Georges Pompidou

FRENCH GUIANA
Devil's Island
Surinam and Brazil
Cayenne

FRENCH POLYNESIA
156
Tahiti
Paul Gauguin

GABON
Albert Schweitzer
Bongo
960

GAMBIA
Banjul
Sir Dawda Jawara
About 500,000

GHANA
The Gold Coast
Kwame Nkrumah
Tema Harbour

Answers

GIBRALTAR
The Calpe
44
1,396 ft

GILBERT ISLANDS
Tuvalu
Christmas Island
Australia

GREECE
Delphi
Rome in 1967
Mikis Theodorakis

GRENADA
The Windward Islands
Genoa
Eric Gairy

GUADELOUPE
Department of France
A monastery in Spain
Guillotine their plantation owners

GUAM
The President of the United States
Agana
The first navigator to sail round the world

GUATEMALA
Chewing gum
The Mayan civilisation
It was destroyed by earthquakes

GUINEA
Three vertical stripes of red, yellow and green
Choose independence outside the French community
Conakry

GUINEA-BISSAU
The oldest European colony in Africa
Portuguese Guinea
General Spinola

GUYANA
Venezuela
Georgetown
Sugar

HAITI
The Comedians
François Duvalier
His son, Jean-Claude, known as 'Baby Doc'

HONDURAS
Over 100
Devastated by Hurricane Fifi
4th–8th centuries

HONG KONG
A British colony
Victoria
1997

HUNGARY
Bela Kun in 1919
Nagy
Magyar

Answers

ICELAND
Denmark
200 miles
No men at all: Iceland has neither an army nor an air force

INDIA
84%
Delhi
Shastri

INDONESIA
Java
Sukarno
Bali

IRAN
Farsi
1941
Omar Khayyam

IRAQ
The Hanging Gardens of Babylon
Assassinated
Dates

IRELAND
1922
Eire
Neutral

ISRAEL
Jordan
Levi Eshkol
Uganda

ITALY
Aldo Moro
Venice
Olive oil

IVORY COAST
Abidjan
Felix Houphouet-Boigny
Establish a dialogue and détente with South Africa

JAMAICA
Oliver Cromwell
Blue Mountains
Queen Elizabeth II

JAPAN
1947 when Japan had a new constitution
The Land of the Rising Sun
Kyoto

JORDAN
Seventeen
His fourth
King Talal

KAMPUCHEA
Cambodia
Prince Sihanouk
Phnom Penh

KENYA
He was arrested after Mau Mau attacks on white farms
They were refused Kenyan citizenship
Nairobi

KUWAIT
United Kingdom
Water
Kuwait

Answers

LAOS
1975
The Pathet Lao
Vientiane

LEBANON
One of the oldest continuously inhabited towns in the world
Pericles, Prince of Tyre
Beirut

LESOTHO
Basutoland
King Moshoeshoe II
Chief Jonathan

LIBERIA
Monrovia
Liberia has a policy of providing a 'flag of convenience' for ships and tankers from many countries
As a country for freed American slaves to live in

LIBYA
The Italians
King Idris
The country's main oil-fields

LIECHTENSTEIN
German
65 square miles
Prince Franz Josef II

LUXEMBOURG
Netherlands
The rose
Letzeburgesch

MADAGASCAR
Mogadisho
The French
Tananarive

MALAWI
Nyasaland
Dr Hastings Banda
Mozambique and Tanzania

MALAYSIA
Sabah
H.R.H. Tunku Yahya Putra Ibni-Marhum Sultan Ibrahim, Sultan of Kelantan
Buddhist

MALDIVE ISLANDS
Over 2,000 of which about 220 are inhabited
A kind of fish
Gan

MALI
French Soudan
Timbuktu
The leader of a dance troupe

MALTA
Comino
The Knights of St John
The George Cross

MAURITANIA
Morocco
Nothing at all, because there is no opposition
Polisario Front

Answers

MAURITIUS
Prince Maurice of Nassau
Sugar
Mauritius rupee

MEXICO
An eagle on a cactus devouring a snake
Popocatepetl
Hernando Cortes

MONACO
Grimaldi
Prince Albert
1956

MONGOLIA
1162 to 1227
Around 1,500,000
Soviet Union

MOROCCO
Bob Hope
King Hassan II
Casablanca

MOZAMBIQUE
Moçambique
Lourenço Marques
Vasco da Gama

NAURU
President Hammer de Roburt
Over 7,000
Phosphates

NEPAL
The Gurkhas
King Mahendra
29,028 ft

NETHERLANDS
The Hague
Eggs
Her mother the Queen abdicated

NEW ZEALAND
Abel Tasman
South Island
7%

NICARAGUA
Lake Nicaragua
Somoza
Managua

NIGER
The Sahara desert
French
Hamani

NIGERIA
Sir Abubakar Tafewa Balewa
Biafra
Ibo

NORTH KOREA
The 38th parallel
1950
Kim Il Sung

NORWAY
The Storting
Denmark
Henrik Ibsen

OMAN
He was deposed by his son
Muscat
Masira

Answers

PAKISTAN
Jinnah
Ayub Khan
Lahore

PANAMA
A hat
1904–1914
General Omar Torrijos

PAPUA NEW GUINEA
Borneo
Indonesia
English

PARAGUAY
General Stroessner
Asuncion
Guarani

PERU
Pizarro
The Inca civilisation
Michael Bentine

PHILIPPINES
20,000,000 dollars
Pilipino (based on Tagalog)
Quezon City

POLAND
His piano playing
Chopin
Copernicus

PORTUGAL
Brazil
Dr Salazar
Oporto

QATAR
Doha
Organisation of Petroleum Exporting Countries
Arabic

RUMANIA
President Ceausescu
Ovid
The Black Sea

RWANDA
Burundi
Germany
A monarch

SAN MARINO
A.D. 301
24
Rimini

SÃO TOMÉ AND PRINCIPÉ
The Gulf of Guinea
1371
The slave trade

SAUDI ARABIA
Assassinated
Saudi Arabia
Mecca

SENEGAL
1840
1960
As a poet

SEYCHELLES
Creole
Mahé
Palms

Answers

SIERRA LEONE
To provide a colony for destitute slaves
'The white man's grave'
Freetown

SINGAPORE
Sir Stamford Raffles
President Benjamin Sheares
54

SOLOMON ISLANDS
The United Kingdom
Honiara
Mountainous and covered with rain forests

SOMALIA
The Horn of Africa
Drought
Soviet Union

SOUTH AFRICA
17%
Jan Smuts
Namibia

SOUTH KOREA
Japan
Syngman Rhee
The won

SOUTH YEMEN
Aden
1967
Communist republic

SOVIET UNION
Union of Soviet Socialist Republics
Nikolay Podgorny
Leo Tolstoy

SPAIN
Sancho Panzo, though Rosinante could also be described as Don Quixote's companion since she was his horse
Stolen from the National Gallery in London
The Cortes

SRI LANKA
1972
Tea, rubber and coconuts
Mrs Bandaranaike

SUDAN
Black
General Gordon
The Union Jack

SURINAM
They received it as a gift from Britain in return for giving Britain what is now New York
Paramaribo
Guyana

SWAZILAND
King Sobhuza II
Emalangeri
Mbabane

SWEDEN
The Gota Canal
As the discoverer of dynamite
Tage Erlander

Answers

SWITZERLAND
Romansch
1971
John Calvin

SYRIA
The Mediterranean Sea
The Golan Heights
Saladin

TAIWAN
Formosa
Chiang Kai-shek
Expelled so that mainland China could have a seat on the Security Council

TANZANIA
Zanzibar
Mount Kilimanjaro
Julius

THAILAND
1350
Deborah Kerr
Bangkok

TOGO
The Lomé Convention
France
Military dictatorship

TONGA
The Friendly Islands
Salote
1643

TRINIDAD AND TOBAGO
Port of Spain
Venezuela
Eric Williams

TUNISIA
Bourguiba
Carthage
The dinar

TURKEY
Constantinople *and* Byzantium
Kemal Ataturk
St Sophia

UGANDA
Alan Coren
Lake Victoria
Kampala

UNITED ARAB EMIRATES
Abu Dhabi
Trucial States
Sunni Muslim

UNITED KINGDOM
50,000
It has never been written down
The Severn

UNITED STATES OF AMERICA
13
Garfield and McKinley
John Adams

Answers

URUGUAY
Montevideo
The smallest country on the continent
The Rio de la Plata which, of course, *is* the River Plate

VATICAN CITY
About 1,000
Castel Gandolfo
Birth control

VENEZUELA
Many people lived in houses built on stilts over water
Simon Bolivar
The Orinoco

VIETNAM
1976
Ho Chi Minh City
The 17th parallel

THE VIRGIN ISLANDS
Britain and the United States
The Panama Canal
About 100

VOLTAIC REPUBLIC
Ivory Coast
France
The Mossi

WEST GERMANY
The German Federal Republic
West Berlin
Konrad Adenauer

WEST INDIES ASSOCIATED STATES
St Kitts in 1623
Christopher Columbus
One of the islands

WESTERN SAHARA
Unsettled
Potash
Polisario

WESTERN SAMOA
Savai'i, Upolou, Manono and Apolima
Robert Louis Stevenson
United States

YEMEN ARAB REPUBLIC
Chairman of Command Council
Cotton
Arabia Felix

YUGOSLAVIA
The Serbs
Josip
Six

ZAÏRE
Kinshasa
June 1960
Kasavubu

Answers

ZAMBIA
Kenneth Kaunda
Livingstone
The Tan-Zam Railway

ZIMBABWE
5%
Zambia
Wankie